# Soup

## VAIBHAV SINHA

INDIA · SINGAPORE · MALAYSIA

## Notion Press

No.8, 3rd Cross Street
CIT Colony, Mylapore
Chennai, Tamil Nadu – 600004

First Published by Notion Press 2020
Copyright © Vaibhav Sinha 2020
All Rights Reserved.

ISBN 978-1-64951-813-2

This book has been published with all efforts taken to make the material error-free after the consent of the author. However, the author and the publisher do not assume and hereby disclaim any liability to any party for any loss, damage, or disruption caused by errors or omissions, whether such errors or omissions result from negligence, accident, or any other cause.

While every effort has been made to avoid any mistake or omission, this publication is being sold on the condition and understanding that neither the author nor the publishers or printers would be liable in any manner to any person by reason of any mistake or omission in this publication or for any action taken or omitted to be taken or advice rendered or accepted on the basis of this work. For any defect in printing or binding the publishers will be liable only to replace the defective copy by another copy of this work then available.

"Adversity introduces a man to himself."

**Albert Einstein**

*Remembering my father:*

Dr Ravindra Nath Sinha

27.08.1942 - 04.09.1994

# CONTENTS

**Disclaimer**: All views expressed in this book are personal. Events, facts and figures contained in this book are taken from publically-available sources. Author or the publisher does a not claim copyright on the images and trademarks used in this book. The author has represented facts with no intent to malign or harm any business interests, individuals, industry, organisation/s, religion, race or sect. Author or the publisher do not assume any responsibility for actions of any individual/s based on the contents of this book. Reader discretion is solicited.

# FOREWORD

Namaskar!

Books and life, both take shape based on our experiences. Unlike books, life, for most of us, does not follow a pre-defined template. Twists and turns are integral to our journey of life; their absence makes life monotonous.

This book is an outcome of a similar twist in our lives, the COVID-19 pandemic, which has impacted each one of us in an unprecedented manner.

Imposition of nationwide lockdown on 24th March, 2020, gave me the extra time to pursue a long-cherished desire of writing a book. This book is an attempt to analyse important developments during the COVID-19 pandemic, flavoured with my perspective and commentary. Due to the dynamic nature of the current situation, some of the facts and figures might change by the time this book is published. Nevertheless, I have taken utmost care in presenting relevant information in appropriate context.

Even after more than eight months into the pandemic, there's no end in sight. So far, we have acclimatized well to the new realities of life. We have to live through this transformation with grit, grace and gratitude. Vagaries of the present could become virtues of the future, if we can assimilate and gain from the experiences of this catharsis.

I express my deep condolences to families who have lost their loved ones to the pandemic. My salute to the numerous doctors, nurses, healthcare and sanitation workers, police personnel and umpteen unknown warriors who are on the frontlines of this global catastrophe.

I thank God Almighty and my Mother for being the reason of my existence and for whatever I am, or have today. Thanks to my better half, Rupali, for her motivation in taking this literary plunge and my chirpy little daughter, Anaisha, for being the cause of immense joy in our lives. Special gratitude to my in-house editorial team, comprising my wife, elder sister and parents-in-law for their valuable suggestions and critique. I'm indebted to my two sisters and brothers-in-law for their guardianship and support.

Thanks to all my family, friends and colleagues for their encouragement and readers who have reposed faith in the content and views expressed in this book.

Last but not the least, thanks to my publisher for their contribution in bringing this book to the readers.

I hope the following pages will make an interesting and insightful read.

With regards,

**Vaibhav Sinha**
20th August, 2020

# INTRODUCTION

On 31$^{st}$ December, 2019, a crowd of a million revellers had gathered underneath the kaleidoscopic sky to witness the New Year's Eve Ball descend atop the One Times Square, New York. It is a tradition celebrated every year since 1907, as the clock nears midnight, to bid adieu to the year gone by and welcome the New Year with joy and hope for better times ahead.

Little did they know, almost simultaneously, a ball-shaped virus was also descending, determined to unleash itself on mankind and change course of human history. The same day, China officially informed the WHO of a cluster of viral pneumonia-like illness with unknown cause in Wuhan city. One month later, the illness was declared a Public Health Emergency of International Concern, which had by then impacted nineteen countries and had close to 8,000 confirmed patients.

The International Committee on Taxonomy of Viruses (ICTV) announced "severe acute respiratory syndrome coronavirus 2 (SARS-CoV-2)" as the name of the new virus on 11$^{th}$ February, 2020. This name was chosen because the virus is genetically related to the coronavirus responsible for the SARS outbreak of 2003. The World Health Organization (WHO) on the same day, named the new disease caused by SARS-CoV-2 as "COVID-19." The COVID-19 acronym stands for corona (CO), virus (VI) and disease (D). Suffix 19 is added to denote the year it was identified.

The name "Coronavirus" is derived from Latin word "corona," meaning "crown" or "wreath," due to the bulbous surface projections which resemble the solar corona or halo. The name was coined by Scottish virologist June Dalziel Almeida, a pioneer in virus imaging, identification, and diagnosis, who first observed and studied human coronaviruses. Her contribution to medical science never got the recognition it deserved during her lifetime, but her research is the backbone of all ongoing efforts to find a cure for COVID-19.

In humans, coronaviruses cause respiratory tract infections that can range from mild to severe. Mild illnesses include some cases of the common cold , while in severe forms it can cause diseases like SARS, MERS and COVID-19. As yet, there are no vaccines or antiviral drugs to prevent or treat human coronavirus infections. Given the severity of COVID-19, many clinical trials are being conducted at break neck speed to identify a vaccine and possible treatment. On 11th August, 2020, Russian President Vladimir Putin announced that a vaccine developed by Moscow's Gamaleya Institute for COVID-19 named Sputnik-V has been given regulatory approval. It is the first vaccine to be approved for COVID-19, although experts have raised concerns about the vaccine's safety and efficacy, given it has not yet entered Phase-3 clinical trials.

COVID-19, was declared a Pandemic on 11th of March, 2020 by the WHO. From its advent in Wuhan towards the end of 2019 until mid-August 2020, COVID-19 virus had traversed the entire globe, infecting more than 22 million people in 200+ countries. It had claimed close to 800,000 lives, and approximately 15 million people have recovered so far. The ultimate number of cases and casualties will only be available once the pandemic is over. For now, it's a race against time, as scientists world over are working tirelessly to discover a vaccine to tame the deadly virus.

In absence of a vaccine or an effective treatment, preventing the spread of the virus is the only effective way of containing the pandemic. It has forced a complete ban on international travel and restrictions on people movement on a global basis. To enforce minimal people to people contact, authorities had to impose national lockdowns, bringing all economic activities to a grinding halt.

More than the disease itself, collateral damage caused by the pandemic is more catastrophic. This pandemic has altered geo-political equations and exposed the inability of global leaders and institutions in managing the challenge at hand. Vulnerability of healthcare systems, in even most advanced countries, to deal with an outbreak of this proportion is out in the open, and so are the fault lines caused by rapid globalisation and dependence on global supply chains. The world is reeling under a global recession of worst kind since The Great Depression of 1930s.

Besides the economic mayhem, it has the potential to alter the demographic and social fabric in many parts of the world. Global economic hubs owe their status to a number of migrants – both national and international.

Due to the pandemic, we have witnessed reverse migration of the worst kind in decades. On one side, migrants will be more cautious in crossing borders for earning a livelihood, and on the other hand, rise in sentiment to secure jobs for locals is expected to make businesses migrant-shy. The world will also see a return of protectionism, in form of trade and non-trade barriers, imposed either as a genuine intent to create more opportunities for locals, or simply, in retaliation to actions by other countries.

Every cloud has a silver lining, and so does COVID-19. Despite the umpteen hardships caused by the pandemic, once it is over, we will witness a transformed new world with a few positives for sure. The biggest beneficiary of COVID- 19 crisis has been Mother Nature, which has always been at the receiving end of rapid industrialisation in the last few decades. Some industries like healthcare and pharmaceuticals have got a new lease of life with enhanced budget allocation and funding, while the hospitality, travel and aviation sector is gasping for survival. As the events unfold, the side-effects of the pandemic are likely to open up more such stories of gloom and bloom.

This pandemic is a rumble strip which shall pass soon, paving the way for a long journey ahead. We are still crossing the early bumps and don't know how long or how many more rumble strips lie ahead.

We won't know either, unless we start the journey.

So, let's begin.

# CHAPTER ONE

## A WHISTLE FROM THE WILD

On 30th December, 2019, Dr Li Wenliang, an Ophthalmologist employed with the Wuhan Central Hospital, stumbled upon a patient's report sent on his WeChat group. The report originated from the director of emergency department of the same hospital where Dr Li worked. It indicated high possibility of SARS coronavirus infection among patients being treated for pneumonia of unknown cause, which had already perturbed doctors due to the unusual spike in cases. Centre for Disease Control (CDC), Wuhan had already alerted hospitals to investigate the exact cause of pneumonia.

Alarmed, Dr Li wrote a WeChat message to his batch mates from the Wuhan University School of Medicine, about seven confirmed cases of SARS being reported from the Huanan Wet market. In continuation, he sent the patient's examination report and CT scan image, confirming that the cases were indeed coronavirus infections of unknown strains. He asked them to inform their family and friends to take precautions, while being discreet on the information shared by him.

Much to his dismay, the chat message he had sent found its way on the internet and was widely circulated in China. He was blamed by the hospital administration for leaking information. Within the same week, he was interrogated by the Wuhan Public Security Bureau. He was issued a warning and was censored for making false comments on the Internet. He was made to sign a letter of apology, promising not to repeat the offence.

Dr Li resumed work shortly after. While treating a glaucoma patient, who had the infection, Dr Li contracted the virus, developed fever and cough, which soon became critical. On 12th January, Li was admitted to the ICU of Wuhan Central Hospital, where he was formally diagnosed with the virus infection on 1st February. His condition became critical four days later and the next day, while speaking to a friend, his oxygen saturation level dropped to 85%. He succumbed the same day, leaving behind a five year old son and a pregnant wife. Despite attempts by Chinese authorities to muzzle his voice and the voices that were raised in his favour, he had become famous for blowing the whistle about the looming threat. He was among the first few of the many corona warriors who laid down their own life while protecting the lives of others.

Dr Li's last moments were closely followed on social media by more than 17 million people. Two days after his death, hundreds of people gathered in Central Park, New York to commemorate his death. The US Senate passed a resolution in his honour, calling for greater transparency by the Chinese Government and Communist Party of China.

The Chinese Government, after being cornered by the public outrage and backlash from international media, honoured Dr Li as a martyr along with thirteen others, mostly physicians who died while treating corona infected patients.

The glaucoma patient whom Dr Li was treating was a storekeeper at the Huanan Wet market with a high viral load. Unconfirmed reports suggest that the virus transitioned from an animal host to a human host in this wet market. Of the initial 41 people hospitalised with pneumonia, who were officially identified as having laboratory-confirmed SARS-CoV-2 infections, two-thirds were exposed to the Huanan Wet market.

Wet markets in China are notorious for selling exotic wild animals such as primates, peacocks, pangolins, wolf pups, civets, crocodiles, snakes, dogs, koalas, turtles bamboo rats, porcupines, live fish and mongoose, et al., packed and stacked on top of each other in cages.

As per WHO estimates, 70% of new viruses originate in animals. It has now been confirmed that in the past, different types of diseases such as AIDS, SARS, Ebola and MERS have originated in wild animals and have transmitted to humans. AIDS and Ebola originated from non-human primates, SARS from bats via civets cats, MERS from bats via camels and SARS-CoV-2 originated in bats and were transmitted to humans via pangolins.

*Wet markets in China ; Source: Google*

In these wet markets, illegally-smuggled wild animals are butchered live. To keep leftover meat fresh, sellers use ice slabs. As the ice melts, blood spreads onto small alleys in the market and hence, the term 'Wet Market.'

Wet markets and consumption of wild animals in China have a cultural and historical significance. Consumption of wildlife in China was confined to the southern part of the country before Mao Zedong implemented the policy of The Great Leap Forward. The aim of this policy, implemented during 1958 to 1962, was to transform China from an agrarian economy into an industrialised one. Mao's focus was on multiplying grain yields and bringing industry to the countryside.

To industrialize, millions of people from farms were moved into iron and steel manufacturing plants, which lowered farm productivity. Mao also believed that sparrows ate too much grain and that was the reason for poor grain yield. He ordered all sparrows to be killed, which is known as the "Smash Sparrow" campaign. Sparrows were shot down or scared away from landing, until they dropped dead of exhaustion. What Mao ignored was the fact that the sparrows ate not just grain, but also locusts and other crop-eating insects. This eventually led to a spike in locust attacks and exponential rise in insect infestations, resulting in low farm yields.

Under pressure from the Communist Party of China to create an illusionary abundance of grains, local officials were forced to collect "surpluses" that, in reality, did not exist, leaving farmers to starve. During this period, an estimated 18-45 million deaths occurred due to starvation, disease and violence. To combat the shortage of food, people started killing and consuming wild animal species, making them scarce in the process and creating a culture of eating wild animals. Subsequent policies by the government triggered a domestication and farming frenzy of wild animals to cope up with increased demand for wild animal meat. This contributed to the creation and growth of wet markets in most parts of China.

Soon after the linkage between the market and infected patients came to light, authorities closed the market to conduct investigations, clean and disinfect the location. However, by mid-April 2020, the Huanan Wet market and many other wet markets in China were back in business. The Chinese Government, on 24th February, banned all trade and consumption of wild animals amidst domestic and international pressure, barring the consumption and trade of wild animals in Traditional Chinese Medicine.

Wet markets remain a prime suspect. However, there is no conclusive evidence that the virus indeed transitioned from an animal host to human hosts, here at the wet markets.

The exact origins of the virus still remain a mystery. The scientific community seems to have reconciled to the fact that it had a natural origin and was not lab-grown as being propagated by some conspiracy theorists. These conspiracy theorists include some prominent figures like the French Nobel laureate Luc Montagnier, US President Donald Trump and his Secretary of State, Mike Pompeo.

At the centre of these claims is the Chinese Institute of Virology located in Wuhan which has three live strains of bat coronavirus on-site. Professor Shi Zhengli and her team has been researching bat coronaviruses since 2004 and focused on the "source tracing of SARS," the strain behind the SARS outbreak in 2003. She claims that the whole genome of SARS-CoV-2 is only 80% similar to that of SARS. A 20% difference in genomic parlance is a highly significant difference. The theory of an accidental leakage of the virus from Wuhan Lab is merely speculative without any scientific explanation, as being concurred by most scientists.

It cannot be completely ruled out either that virus outbreaks cannot happen due to laboratory accidents. Such accidents are not uncommon, as happened in case of SARS in 2003-04 when three outbreaks within a span of one year were caused due to failure in laboratory containment at the Chinese Institute of Virology in Beijing. A similar outbreak happened in Singapore, at the Environmental Health Institute when a doctoral student of West Nile virus was infected with SARS due to cross contamination of West Nile virus samples with SARS coronavirus samples in the laboratory.

Some experts like Dr Robert Garry, a professor at the Tulane University School of Medicine, even doubt the theory that virus originated in Huanan Wet market. He believes, the cause of pandemic could be a mutation in surface proteins of the virus which could have occurred over a period of time.

Be that as it may, there is no conclusive scientific evidence yet to prove the actual origins of the virus; whether it mutated naturally, grown in a lab or accidentally escaped the lab. It may take several years before scientists are able to identify the origins of COVID-19 virus. It was not until 2015, i.e. thirteen years after the SARS outbreak, when scientists were able to identify horseshoe bats as the natural host of the virus. It took more than eighty years to identify the cause of Spanish Flu.

If past outbreaks are any indication, in most cases, the viruses have transmitted to humans from a wild animal host. One of the reasons for frequent outbreaks of viruses in Asia and Africa is the rapid urbanization, where sixty percent of the world already lives. Deforestation caused by expansion of cities and need for agricultural land has led to humans eating into the natural habitats of wild animals (and in some cases, even eating them!). Such outbreaks are likely to increase in the future as humans get closer to the wild.

Dr Li blew the whistle on the pandemic, but it is even more important to listen to the whistle coming from the wild, in form of these recurring virus outbreaks. Nature is alarming us to mind our steps, which are increasingly in conflict with it.

The message is loud and clear – Let us not smash our sparrows again!

# CHAPTER TWO

## THE PANDEMIC

WHO declared COVID-19, a global health emergency on 30th January, 2020, which was later upgraded to a Pandemic status on the 11th March, 2020.

The majority of global population, only familiar with social networks until then, woke up to a new reality of life – Social Distancing. Since COVID-19 virus spreads via close contact between an infected and a healthy individual, in absence of a vaccine and treatment for the disease, social distancing is the most potent tool in tackling the pandemic. Rapid spread of the virus across continents and countries, created a global health scare, drawing comparisons with the Spanish Flu pandemic of 1918 which claimed more than 50 million lives and affected 500 million people i.e. a quarter of the global population at the time. As the name suggests, Spanish Flu had nothing to do with Spain. It was just one of the affected countries. It got the name as Spain was a neutral country during World War I and had a free press. People world over only read news coming out of Spain about the pandemic and hence, it was associated with Spain.

One may ask, "What's the fuss about the name?" We shall find later.

*The Spanish Flu, 1918 ; Source: Google*

The Spanish Flu of 1918-20 lasted for about eighteen months and erupted in three phases. The first phase started when a cook employed at an army camp in Kansas was hospitalized with high fever. Thereafter, the virus spread to 54,000 troops, hospitalising 11,000 of them and causing 38 fatalities after developing pneumonia. Via the troops, it then reached Europe, spreading like wildfire to England, France, Italy and Spain. French and English troops were the worst affected, as three fourths of the French and half of the English troops were infected. The first wave was not so deadly, as it only caused high fever, lasted three days and had mortality rates similar to the seasonal flu. By early August 1918, cases dropped, raising hopes of an end to the Spanish flu.

It proved to be the lull before the storm. The second phase erupted in Europe via ships from British ports, unknowingly carrying infected troops to France, US and Africa. The virus had mutated by then, emerging deadlier than before. It could infect healthy young adults and kill them within twenty four hours of being infected. The second phase was known by the "W Curve," indicating that it did not just infect the very old and very young, but infected the healthier adults aged 25-35, indicated by the middle spike in letter "W." The second phase lasted from September- November 1918.

What made the second phase deadly was not the fatality alone but also the way it killed the victims. The virus strain caused a phenomenon called "cytokine explosion." When under attack from a virus, the body immune system activates proteins called cytokines. It triggered an immune response, causing overload of cytokines. Victims would develop fever and breathlessness. The lack of oxygen would turn the face blue. Haemorrhages filled the lungs with blood, causing vomiting, nosebleeds and choking the victim to death. Such damage to the lungs, was akin to the one caused by chemical weapons.

The second wave of the Spanish flu was fast and furious, killing millions, before subsiding towards the end of December, 1918. It emerged again in January 1919 in Australia, from where it spread back to Europe and the US. This was the third wave of Spanish Flu which was equally high in number of fatalities, but was less gruesome than the second wave.

The Spanish Flu, caused more than 200,000 deaths in England. In the US, the death toll was close to 700,000 and Japan, 400,000. Western Samoa lost one fifth of its population, and estimates reveal that in India alone, close to twenty million people died. Spanish Flu killed more people than the two world wars combined.

Thankfully, medical science and healthcare infrastructure is much advanced and accessible now than it was a hundred years ago. That said, it is also much easier for the virus to spread now, as we live in a more physically-connected world, have more avenues for social interactions and faster modes of transport. Back then, citizens were ordered to wear masks, and schools, theatres and businesses were shut. People were incentivised to wear masks and follow social distancing norms. Unfortunately, despite advances in medical science and other fields, we are no better than our ancestors when it comes to prevention or treatment of the disease. They had no vaccine or cure. They had to be trained, admonished and incentivised to wear masks and adhere to social distancing norms. So do we. At least, for now, our options to prevent spread of the virus are no different than they were a hundred years ago.

Scale and scare of the COVID-19 pandemic can be gauged from the fact that more than one third of global population went into a complete lockdown by the 31st March, 2020. International borders were closed, most leading world monuments still remain out of bounds to public and all international flight movement (except those ferrying stranded citizens of various countries) came to a grinding halt.

Tokyo Olympics 2020 has been postponed to 2021, and so are other major entertainment, political, social or sporting events. With schools and colleges closed, kids are learning virtually, while their parents are working from the confines of their homes. The less fortunate have no work at all. Among them, some are surviving on government aids and the others are feeding themselves a mere hope of an end to the pandemic.

At a time when the world is bickering over economic status, race, religion, region and colour, the pandemic has proven to be a great leveller. Without discrimination of any sorts, it has impacted the meek and mighty alike – the Saudi Royal Family, Prince of Wales, the British PM, the Russian PM, the Brazilian President, India's Home Minister, the

Ex PM of Pakistan, the First Lady of Canada, and wife of the Spanish PM are some of the leading global politicians who were infected. Hollywood actor Tom Hanks and his wife, actress and singer Rita Wilson, British actor Idris Elba, singer Pink and opera singer Placido Domingo are some of the best-known celebrities who were infected. So did Bollywood superstar of the millennium, Amitabh Bachchan along with his actor son Abhishek, daughter-in-law and former Miss World Aishwarya Rai and his granddaughter, Aradhya. The world's No. 1 tennis player, Novak Djokovic and Shahid Afridi, the ex-cricketer from Pakistan were among the several sportspersons of repute who had contracted the viral infection. Some prominent faces who succumbed to the pandemic include Alan Merrill, the performer and songwriter famous for the hit 'I Love Rock 'n' Roll,' Ken Shimura, one of Japan's best-known comedians and Floyd Cardoz, the celebrity chef and winner of Season Three of the US show Top Chef Masters, besides many others worldwide.

By mid-August 2020, the pandemic had infected close to 22 million people and claimed more than 800,000 lives worldwide. The numbers kept increasing each passing day with countries displacing each other to claim prime spot on the not-so-coveted COVID-19 charts. On 28th February, 2020, China and South Korea were the first and second worst affected countries respectively. By 31st March, 2020, USA and Italy replaced the two. While the US maintained its lead as the worst affected, other top five spots saw Italy, Brazil, Russia, UK, India, Spain, France, Iran, South Africa and Peru, jostling to replace each other.

Wuhan, the initial epicentre of the pandemic, gradually returned to normal, but the virus had by then engulfed 200+ countries. Galloping number of cases each passing day turned the pandemic into a contest of sorts with nations vying with other to top the charts of number of cases. Countries with a high population density, such as India, Bangladesh, Pakistan, Brazil, Peru, Chile and Indonesia caught up fast with their counterparts in the developed world, as testing gained pace and the virus spread to community clusters.

The initial low number of cases per million in the developing world turned out to be just the tip of an iceberg. Their initial low numbers were due to the limitations in access to health care centres, low testing rates and the fact that the virus outbreak started late, giving them the opportunity to put a huge number of people under lockdowns. Once the lockdowns were eased, cases grew exponentially.

China on the other hand, has been largely successful in containing the pandemic to its epicentre in Wuhan, and was able to control the outbreak by mid-April. Emergency hospitals in Wuhan were dismantled, and most of the corona warriors brought in to deal with the unprecedented high number of cases had retreated to their base stations.

Despite the early success, China remains vulnerable to the pandemic. As it was gradually returning to normal, cases spiked, caused by overseas travellers who returned to China and from wet markets which reopened. On 12th June, 2020 eleven residential complexes in Beijing were sealed after a fresh cluster of coronavirus cases emerged in the city. Six cases of coronavirus were linked to the local Xinfadi beef and lamb market. New, domestically-transmitted cases were also reported from Xinjiang province in early August, prompting the authorities to declare it in a 'wartime situation' and putting it under complete lockdown.

South Korea, which was among the early success stories due to their COVID-19 testing and tracking methods, confirmed second wave of pandemic in the country on 22nd June, 2020. Clusters of new cases grew, including outbreaks at nightclubs in the capital Seoul, forcing health authorities to implement more stringent measures to ensure social distancing and containment. On 25th July, South Korea reported the highest single daily spike in new cases since March 2020. Most of these cases were imported infections, found among construction workers airlifted from war-ravaged Iraq.

COVID-19 challenged the otherwise-impeccable healthcare systems in even the most advanced countries. The influx of patients caused extreme shortage of ventilators, ICU beds and Personal Protective Equipment (PPE) required to protect healthcare workers and doctors from contracting the infection. Stories of several doctors and nurses, healthcare workers and police personnel, succumbing to the virus became a routine feature. In some developing countries, doctors and nurses had to attend to patients even without the PPE kits. Ingenious people came up with innovative alternatives – raincoats and garbage bags doubled up as PPE kits in many instances!

The priority of governments and policy makers during the initial days of the pandemic was to contain further spread by imposing complete lockdowns and channelizing all resources in treatment and care of severely ill patients. Stadiums, banquets halls, schools and even train coaches were converted into isolation and treatment centres. Due to the contagious nature of the virus, despite drastic measures by governments, the number of cases steadily increased. 'Flatten the curve' became the buzz word among healthcare strategists at all levels, be it global, national, provincial or municipal.

As the world grappled with rapid virus spread from country by country, policy makers had the challenge to deal with the collateral damage caused by the near global shutdown of economic activity. Economic impact of the pandemic was further exacerbated by the fact that Top 5 affected countries, US, Brazil, Russia, India and UK*, are also leading global economies that contribute more than one third of the global GDP. The IMF has already declared that we are in a global recession. World bank's Global Economic Prospects report of June 2020 estimates that the global economy will contract by 5.2% in 2020 due to the pandemic. Almost all countries were expected to plunge into a recession, reducing per capita GDP in highest number of countries since 1870.

* UK was replaced by Peru as the 5th worst affected country by end August.

Socio-economic compulsions have pushed nations to relax restrictions on people movement and business activity. By mid-2020, most countries had eased restrictions, albeit with certain caveats. Some of the worst-affected countries like Spain even opened itself to tourists from within Europe. In India, migrants living in metro cities were allowed to go back to their home town in specially-run trains and buses. As the crowded trains rolled on tracks, thousands of migrant labours and workers moved to their home towns, often flouting social distancing norms. It's difficult to fathom that the migrants were all alone in their journey back home and didn't carry the virus along. The rise in cases from the country side tells the tale.

It is hard to say if we are riding a wave or floating in a deluge. As nations attempt return to pre COVID-19 era, the odds of a second wave with even higher number of cases cannot be ruled out. The resumption of international travel, opening up of theatres, educational institutions, malls, beaches, sports complexes and restaurants are going to be the likely source of a second wave of virus outbreak. At these places, people tend to be more casual and are likely to flout social distancing norms. Recent cases in China, South Korea and New Zealand indicate that the threat of a second or even a third wave of the pandemic is real.

The WHO has been warning that we have to learn to live with the virus. It is not going to end any time soon. Even when the vaccine is available, it is practically impossible to administer it to entire eight billion people living on the planet, which is the only way to annihilate the virus completely. Since that is not the case, the virus will live with us, occasionally making a few sick, sometimes very sick. Natural immunity, effective treatments and most importantly, change in human behaviour is what will end the pandemic.

Hope is a good thing, and good things never die.

| # | Country | Total Cases | Total Deaths | Total Recovered | Active Cases | Total Cases per million | Deaths per million | Total Tests | Tests per million | Population |
|---|---|---|---|---|---|---|---|---|---|---|
| | World | 22,189,166 | 780,399 | 14,901,055 | 6,507,712 | 2,847 | 100 | 394,158,453 | 50,741 | 7,768,057,606 |
| 1 | USA | 5,627,618 | 174,293 | 2,981,277 | 2,472,048 | 16,989 | 526 | 71,909,498 | 217,081 | 331,256,357 |
| 2 | Brazil | 3,370,262 | 108,900 | 2,478,494 | 782,868 | 15,841 | 512 | 13,729,872 | 64,533 | 212,756,034 |
| 3 | India | 2,766,626 | 53,023 | 2,035,143 | 678,460 | 2,002 | 38 | 30,941,264 | 22,393 | 1,381,752,440 |
| 4 | Russia | 932,493 | 15,872 | 742,628 | 173,993 | 6,389 | 109 | 32,968,759 | 225,902 | 145,942,798 |
| 5 | South Africa | 589,886 | 11,982 | 477,671 | 100,233 | 9,930 | 202 | 3,415,670 | 57,499 | 59,404,038 |
| 6 | Peru | 541,493 | 26,481 | 370,717 | 144,295 | 16,394 | 802 | 2,793,614 | 84,578 | 33,030,127 |
| 7 | Mexico | 525,733 | 57,023 | 359,347 | 109,363 | 4,072 | 442 | 1,181,695 | 9,153 | 129,106,847 |
| 8 | Colombia | 476,660 | 15,372 | 301,525 | 159,763 | 9,355 | 302 | 2,259,743 | 44,350 | 50,952,553 |
| 9 | Chile | 388,855 | 10,546 | 362,440 | 15,869 | 20,319 | 551 | 2,068,079 | 108,065 | 19,137,440 |
| 10 | Spain | 384,270 | 28,670 | N/A | N/A | 8,218 | 613 | 7,955,615 | 170,147 | 46,757,191 |
| 11 | Iran | 347,835 | 19,972 | 300,881 | 26,982 | 4,134 | 237 | 2,914,049 | 34,637 | 84,129,933 |
| 12 | UK | 320,286 | 41,381 | N/A | N/A | 4,715 | 609 | 14,825,051 | 218,231 | 67,932,724 |
| 13 | Saudi Arabia | 301,323 | 3,470 | 272,911 | 24,942 | 8,638 | 99 | 4,378,417 | 125,520 | 34,882,225 |
| 14 | Argentina | 299,126 | 5,877 | 223,531 | 69,718 | 6,611 | 130 | 994,942 | 21,988 | 45,249,337 |
| 15 | Pakistan | 289,832 | 6,190 | 270,009 | 13,633 | 1,309 | 28 | 2,317,213 | 10,465 | 221,424,972 |
| 16 | Bangladesh | 282,344 | 3,740 | 162,825 | 115,779 | 1,712 | 23 | 1,378,819 | 8,362 | 164,900,676 |
| 17 | Italy | 254,636 | 35,405 | 204,142 | 15,089 | 4,212 | 586 | 7,642,059 | 126,420 | 60,449,906 |
| 18 | Turkey | 251,805 | 6,016 | 232,913 | 12,876 | 2,982 | 71 | 5,882,406 | 69,651 | 84,455,591 |
| 19 | Germany | 227,899 | 9,305 | 202,900 | 15,694 | 2,719 | 111 | 9,265,361 | 110,540 | 83,819,291 |
| 20 | France | 221,267 | 30,429 | 84,065 | 106,773 | 3,389 | 466 | 6,000,000 | 91,894 | 65,292,634 |
| 21 | Iraq | 184,709 | 6,056 | 131,840 | 46,833 | 4,580 | 150 | 1,304,331 | 32,339 | 40,333,218 |
| 22 | Philippines | 169,213 | 2,687 | 112,861 | 53,665 | 1,542 | 24 | 2,108,597 | 19,210 | 109,766,558 |
| 23 | Indonesia | 143,043 | 6,277 | 96,306 | 40,460 | 522 | 23 | 1,915,039 | 6,992 | 273,895,240 |
| 24 | Canada | 123,046 | 9,042 | 109,308 | 4,696 | 3,256 | 239 | 4,840,043 | 128,094 | 37,784,956 |
| 25 | Qatar | 115,368 | 193 | 112,088 | 3,087 | 41,088 | 69 | 555,970 | 198,009 | 2,807,805 |
| 26 | Kazakhstan | 103,300 | 1,269 | 84,445 | 17,586 | 5,493 | 67 | 2,291,327 | 121,844 | 18,805,415 |
| 27 | Ecuador | 102,941 | 6,105 | 87,183 | 9,653 | 5,823 | 345 | 289,213 | 16,361 | 17,676,881 |
| 28 | Bolivia | 101,223 | 4,123 | 37,471 | 59,629 | 8,657 | 353 | 216,774 | 18,538 | 11,693,245 |
| 29 | Egypt | 96,590 | 5,173 | 60,651 | 30,766 | 942 | 50 | 135,000 | 1,316 | 102,574,622 |
| 30 | Israel | 96,093 | 705 | 71,971 | 23,417 | 10,448 | 77 | 2,079,941 | 226,140 | 9,197,590 |
| 31 | Ukraine | 94,436 | 2,116 | 48,925 | 43,395 | 2,161 | 48 | 1,315,409 | 30,102 | 43,698,003 |
| 32 | Dominican Repu | 86,737 | 1,481 | 54,108 | 31,148 | 7,985 | 136 | 324,463 | 29,872 | 10,861,915 |
| 33 | Sweden | 85,219 | 5,790 | N/A | N/A | 8,431 | 573 | 917,036 | 90,728 | 10,107,485 |
| 34 | China | 84,871 | 4,634 | 79,642 | 595 | 59 | 3 | 90,410,000 | 62,814 | 1,439,323,776 |
| 35 | Oman | 83,418 | 597 | 77,977 | 4,844 | 16,285 | 117 | 309,212 | 60,365 | 5,122,362 |
| 36 | Panama | 82,543 | 1,788 | 55,845 | 24,910 | 19,092 | 414 | 273,685 | 63,304 | 4,323,325 |
| 37 | Belgium | 78,534 | 9,944 | 18,003 | 50,587 | 6,772 | 858 | 2,008,070 | 173,165 | 11,596,251 |
| 38 | Kuwait | 77,470 | 505 | 69,243 | 7,722 | 18,107 | 118 | 568,440 | 132,858 | 4,278,558 |
| 39 | Romania | 72,208 | 3,074 | 33,135 | 35,999 | 3,757 | 160 | 1,542,094 | 80,233 | 19,220,188 |
| 40 | Belarus | 69,673 | 617 | 67,339 | 1,717 | 7,374 | 65 | 1,429,532 | 151,291 | 9,448,908 |
| 41 | UAE | 64,906 | 366 | 57,909 | 6,631 | 6,552 | 37 | 6,121,609 | 617,990 | 9,905,669 |
| 42 | Netherlands | 63,973 | 6,175 | N/A | N/A | 3,732 | 360 | 1,312,787 | 76,592 | 17,139,892 |
| 43 | Guatemala | 62,944 | 2,389 | 51,530 | 9,025 | 3,505 | 133 | 200,984 | 11,193 | 17,956,873 |
| 44 | Poland | 57,876 | 1,896 | 39,643 | 16,337 | 1,529 | 50 | 2,409,394 | 63,671 | 37,841,061 |
| 45 | Singapore | 55,938 | 27 | 52,533 | 3,378 | 9,552 | 5 | 1,610,906 | 275,072 | 5,856,313 |
| 46 | Japan | 55,667 | 1,099 | 41,196 | 13,372 | 440 | 9 | 1,186,468 | 9,385 | 126,424,274 |
| 47 | Portugal | 54,448 | 1,784 | 39,936 | 12,728 | 5,342 | 175 | 1,799,226 | 176,521 | 10,192,704 |
| 48 | Honduras | 50,995 | 1,583 | 7,450 | 41,962 | 5,138 | 160 | 123,539 | 12,448 | 9,924,442 |
| 49 | Nigeria | 49,485 | 977 | 36,834 | 11,674 | 239 | 5 | 352,625 | 1,705 | 206,760,319 |
| 50 | Bahrain | 47,185 | 175 | 43,529 | 3,481 | 27,618 | 102 | 981,208 | 574,324 | 1,708,457 |
| | Others | 1,174,865 | 27,825 | 852,886 | 294,154 | 646 | 15 | 38,403,405 | 21,110 | 1,819,198,187 |

Source : Worldometer

# CHAPTER THREE

## DENIALS, DEARTH AND DESPERATION

Just two month prior to the first few cases of COVID-19 being reported from China, Johns Hopkins Centre for Health Security, the Nuclear Threat Initiative (NTI) and the Economist Intelligence Unit (EIU) jointly published the first-ever Global Health Security Index in October 2019. The report contained detailed assessment of health security capabilities in 195 countries. Underlying conclusion of the study was that "no country is fully prepared for epidemics or pandemics, and every country has important gaps to address."

The study was partially right. One may ask, why partially right?

With a score of 83.5 on a scale of 100, US was supposedly the best prepared to deal with a pandemic. Within six months, the myth was shattered. As on 8th August, 2020, the US accounted for a quarter of global cases and the death toll. Higher-ranked UK, Spain and Brazil were caught napping. As the virus unleashed, Vietnam, a country ranked 50 on the index, fared much better.

The report, co-funded by Bill and Melinda Gates foundation, was correct in its assessment of pandemic preparedness by countries like Thailand, Malaysia,

Singapore, Sweden and South Korea. Echoing the index rankings, these countries have, by and large, successfully tamed the virus. Countries called out for their poor pandemic preparedness in the report – Russia, Pakistan, India, Bangladesh and Indonesia – have not disappointed authors of the report either.

The US President repeatedly dismissed early intelligence in January and February about the looming threat from COVID-19. Displaying brazen ignorance and arrogance, he asked the intelligence officials briefing the Congress on the issue to "go back to school." In its annual briefings, the Directorate of National Intelligence (DNI), had repeatedly warned about the risk of a global pandemic, having first raised it in 2009, when President Obama had just taken over, highlighting its impact on human lives and economy. In March 2013, James Clapper, the then Head of DNI, even pointed to the growing danger posed by zoonotic viruses, detailing its potential to spread, mortality and type of illnesses it may cause with eerie similarity to COVID-19, terming it a global pandemic. Clapper's successor predicted a similar threat in May 2017 and repeated the warning in 2019, highlighting its impact on global economy. In another report published in 2008, the threat of a global pandemic was detailed quite accurately, pointing towards it's possible origins in China or South East Asia, and it spreading across continents via global travellers.

President Trump preferred to conveniently ignore those early warnings, remaining in denial for weeks and kept downplaying the outbreak. Until mid-March, he flip flopped, one day, calling it similar to a regular flu, the other day "We have it under control" and a few days later, "We got it down to zero." It was only on 17th March, that he realised the gravity of situation, describing the virus as a highly-contagious "invisible enemy" and declared tough social distancing guidelines. Too less, too late.

In the US, initial testing rates were relatively much lower than countries like South Korea. Both countries reported their first cases on 20th January, 2020. The US has a population seven times that of South Korea. By mid-March, the US had only conducted 60,000 tests as compared to 300,000 by South Korea.

In the third week of January, WHO had published a protocol from German researchers with necessary instructions for any country to manufacture coronavirus tests kits. Still, the US administration decided to use their own testing kits, developed based on CDC protocol, citing 'acceptable standards of quality' to be used on American patients!

The arrogance of a few cost many Americans dearly.

The CDC ended up supplying faulty testing kits to state public-health labs, which as per reports, wrongly-detected the new coronavirus in samples of laboratory-grade water! Replacing the faulty kits and sending samples back to CDC for testing cost the Americans six crucial weeks in pandemic response.

Another fault line in the US approach has been the subtle racism and indifference, which prevails in American society towards Black Americans. Blacks are 13% of total

US population, but make 23% of US death toll caused by the pandemic. Poor living conditions, lack of adequate medical aid, prevalence of comorbidities, lesser testing centres in black neighbourhoods and the sub-conscious partisan attitude of healthcare professionals are being attributed as reasons behind high death toll among Black Americans. As per an independent analysis of data of COVID-19 patients from Washington and 43 other states, the mortality rate was highest among Black Americans. For Black Americans, it stood at 61.6 per 100,000, compared to 36 for Indigenous, 28.2 for Latino, 26.3 for Asians and 26 for White Americans.

Sub-conscious racism in America against Black Americans came to fore with the killing of George Floyd, a 46-year-old black man's in Minneapolis, Minnesota on the 25th May, 2020. Floyd was arrested for allegedly using a counterfeit bill. Derek Chauvin, a white police officer, knelt on Floyd's neck for almost nine minutes, as he kept begging for his life, struggling to breathe. Despite repeated requests by bystanders to remove his knees, Chauvin didn't relent and did so only when the medics arrived. By that time, Floyd had lost his pulse and was lying motionless. He later succumbed to asphyxia.

All four officers involved in the arrest were fired, and Chauvin charged for second degree murder. Floyd's death caused protests across the US, Europe and other parts of the world.

On 23rd June, 2020, Dr Anthony Fauci, the White House health advisor, in a testimony to the Congress admitted that institutional racism has contributed to disproportionate impact of the outbreak on Black Americans. He also acknowledged that the community has suffered racism for a very long period of time, contributing to their poor economic status. This acknowledgement can go a long way in changing the status quo in world's oldest democracy. George Floyd's unfortunate end could be the beginning of a new social revolution in the US.

Down south, the right wing Brazilian President, Jair Bolsonaro's response to the pandemic was equally clumsy. He dismissed it as "little flu" and ridiculed state officials for imposing lockdowns. In mid-April, he fired the then Health Minister, Luiz Henrique Mandetta over disagreements about social distancing guidelines. In less than a month into the job, Luiz successor Health Minister, Nelson Teich, quit, citing reasons similar to his predecessor.

Brazil reported its first COVID-19 case at the end of February. But it failed to take tough containment measures to track and trace the patients at the early stage. It was not until mid-March when community transmission occurred in Sao Paulo and Rio de Janeiro, that governments at all levels began to pay attention. Yet, the authorities were averse to shutting down businesses. As a result, the virus had spread to poor communities.

By June end, when the curve was flattening in many countries in Europe and South East Asia, it continued to rise in Brazil. In some areas, ICU occupancy levels were more than 90%. Despite the surge in cases, many Brazilian states and cities had begun easing quarantine restrictions and reopening businesses.

As the nation was busy digging graves after graves in land tracts meant for cultivation, its President continued to advocate relaxations in lockdown amidst crowded gatherings, standing unmasked and violating all social distancing norms. His callousness cost the country of 200 million people heavily. By August, it stood just behind the US with close to three and a half million cases and more than 100,000 reported deaths, with cases still on the rise.

Experts opined that limited testing capacity and insufficient medical resources were the key reasons behind high infection rates in Brazil. They seemed to have left out the biggest cause, out of courtesy, i.e. President Bolsonaro himself!

Bolsonaro tested positive in early July. He took a month to recover, after making a hat trick testing positive.

Russian response to the pandemic has been somewhat similar to US and Brazil – grossly mismanaged. It is the fourth worst-affected country worldwide with more than 900,000 cases and death toll close to 16,000. The authoritarian regime of President Putin was more focused on the referendum which was conducted between 25th June and 1st July, 2020 – the referendum to bring in constitutional changes that gave sanctity to his presidency until 2036.

Officials have been trying hard to camouflage the actual number of cases, which experts believe could be three times more than what is being reported. People, although aware of the misleading government numbers, are tight lipped due to the strict monitoring of communication and consequences thereof. At the crucial time of the referendum, the risk-averse leadership in Russia has left local administrations to take centre stage, while trying to avoid blame for any failures during the pandemic.

Preoccupied with Brexit and the economic fallout, the UK delayed the lockdown and paid with a steep rise in death numbers. Fresh from the election win in December 2019, Prime Minister Boris Johnson was away on holiday with his fiancée when the pandemic was in its initial leg. He was among the first global leaders to be infected, although he was back in office after spending considerable time in the ICU.

Complacency had cost the country dear. A country ranked second for their pandemic preparedness until a few months back stares at one of the highest death tolls in Europe with close to 41,000 deaths. During the early days of the pandemic, the UK made a grave mistake of ignoring WHO's advice to follow the strategy of testing, isolating and contact tracing. Jenny Harries, England's deputy chief medical officer, was quoted saying that the UK didn't need to follow the WHO advice – "The clue with the WHO is in its title – it's a World Health Organization, and it is addressing all countries across the world." Over confident Jenny!

They relied on the premise of developing herd immunity. In reality, people lost immunity in hordes.

Some countries, however, acted swiftly, but defied logic. Peru announced only men can leave their houses on Mondays, Wednesdays, and Fridays and in Panama, those were the days for women to hang out.

In India, the Government, aware of its fragile health infrastructure and the mammoth population of 1.3 billion, announced a complete lockdown on 24th March, 2020. Five months into it, lockdowns still continue, albeit with some relaxations. Due to timely imposition of lockdown, it did fairly well initially, with much lower cases as compared to the West and its peers in the developing world until a group of Islamic preachers, known as the Tabhlighi Jamaat comprising several foreign nationals, were found to have attended a religious congregation and later, travelled to seventeen states of the country, transmitting the virus all along. The group of believers were not ready to believe that COVID-19 is a life threatening ailment which can spread by spitting and close contact. They resisted authorities and healthcare workers in their efforts to quarantine and treat them. As a result, 30% of close to 14,000 + reported cases in India by the third week of April, traced its origins to the group.

India, despite the lowest number of per million cases, is the third worst-affected country with more than 2.8 million cases and 53,000 deaths so far. Although it witnessed huge spike in daily cases towards July and August, a silver lining for the country is its recovery rate of close to 75%, and a mortality rate of 1.9%, which are much better than the global average of 67% and 3.5 %, respectively.

In neighbouring Pakistan, the Tablighi Jamaat held a congregation on 10th March, 2020 at their country headquarters in Raiwind, Lahore. It became a super spreader event, causing over 2,000 or 27% of the country's reported cases by the end of April.

The situation had turned so alarming by June that WHO, in an unprecedented move, had to recommend re-imposition of lockdown in Pakistan. Prime Minister Imran Khan had unwillingly imposed lockdown in Pakistan on 24th March, 2020, only to be relaxed by the Supreme Court taking "suo motu" cognizance. The honourable court believed that COVID-19 virus was apparently not a pandemic in Pakistan and questioned the funds being spent to fight the pandemic!

Between extremes of a complacent West and ill-equipped developing world, lie countries such as Australia, China, Japan, New Zealand, Singapore, South Korea, Taiwan, Thailand and Vietnam, which have largely been successful in containing the disease spread. Each of them offers useful insights in tackling the menace. In Wuhan, China erected a fully-equipped hospital in ten days flat, showing its exemplary political will and preparedness in tackling the virus outbreak, while Singapore's unique combination of factors, such as a top-notch health system, draconian tracing and containment measures, and a population that followed government's expansive directives, helped in containing the spread to manageable proportions. Korean experience highlights the importance of SOPs, people engagement and the role of individual consciousness of their social responsibilities in infection control. Despite its close proximity to China, high population density and a large aged population, Japan was initially able to control the disease spread which can be attributed to the Japanese culture of hygiene and social etiquette. Wearing masks is quite common and part of the Japanese culture.

Despite being a pariah at the WHO, Taiwan's response to the pandemic has been exemplary. It has effectively used cell phone tracking, big data and mandatory temperature checks (starting as early as 31st December, 2019) to keep the numbers of infected persons strikingly low. Taiwan's transparent dealing with the pandemic and willingness to help and share information, earned it international praise and attention.

When in war, your arms, armour and ammunition decide the outcome. Unfortunately, in the war against COVID-19, most countries had to race against time to ensure availability of arms – Health Care Workers, Nurses and Doctors, armour-Personnel Protective Equipment (PPE) such as masks, facial shield, gloves, etc. and ammunition- testing kits, ventilators, medicines and ICU beds. As per initial estimates, close to 900,000 ventilators were required to cope up with the expected surge in demand. N95 masks recommended for healthcare professionals in close contact with patients were in acute shortage, pushing them to use normal surgical masks, which put them in risk of infection.

At start of the outbreak, the US had twelve million N95 respirators and thirty million surgical masks in its Strategic National Stockpile, which accounted for a meagre 1% of the country's need in a full-blown pandemic. Hand sanitizers, which were not even considered an essential supply item, went out of all supermarkets. As most of these items were predominantly manufactured in China, the shutdown of manufacturing activity there clubbed with its captive needs and sudden global surge in demand, led to an acute shortage of these essential items. When the pandemic began, half of the N95 masks used globally were being made and supplied by China.

Dearth of ICU beds and healthcare professionals to treat COVID-19 patients can be gauged from the fact that in Italy and Spain, in two countries with highest death toll by mid-April, doctors were forced to take possibly the worst decision of their lives – whom to save and whom to let die.

Shortages were not just limited to hospital resources and supplies. In countries with high death toll, even morgues and graveyards ran out of space. Bracing up for the worst and taking cue from Italy and Spain experience, Pakistan acquired eighty acre land near its financial capital of Karachi for a dedicated graveyard for COVID-19 victims. It was the first country to do so. Brazil and Turkey followed suit.

US dug up mass graves in Bronx Island to bury its dead. In March, in city of Qom in Iran, the mass grave site expansion was even visible from space. Images of Army trucks carrying coffins of dead citizens in Italy will remain etched in public memory for long.

Most grisly tale came from Ecuador, where the dead bodies in Guayaquil, its largest and worst affected city, were lying abandoned in busy hospitals or left decomposing inside homes and in extreme cases, even wrapped in plastic and cardboard and put out on the streets!

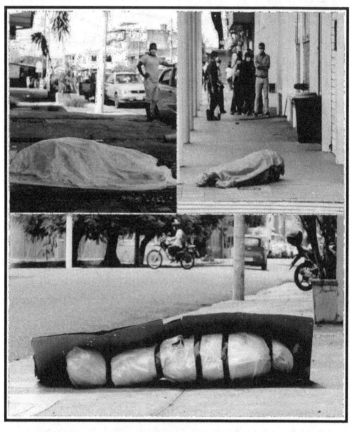

*Dead bodies of COVID-19 victims left on the road in Guayaquil, Ecuador ; Source: Google*

*Dug up mass graves in Iran and Brazil ; Source: Google*

Most countries banned religious ceremonies and large gatherings at the funerals of COVID-19 victims. The pandemic also exposed the dark side of human behaviour when presented with adverse situations. Out of fear of being infected, many close relatives of COVID-19 victims did not turn to claim their bodies, leaving them at the mercy of authorities to find a final resting place.

Desperate times call for desperate measures. To ensure implementation of lockdown, Philippines threatened with shoot at sight orders for violators, while in Saudi Arabia, a man infected with the virus, who was accused of spitting on shopping trolleys, is likely to face capital punishment. Engineers in Italy resorted to combating ventilator shortage by turning snorkelling masks into breathing equipment. In the UK, the Government reached out to the automotive and aviation sectors for making ventilators. In India and the US, fashion designers converted their design studios into workshops, making masks. To cope of with the shortage in initial days of the pandemic, universities started making hand sanitizers in chemistry labs.

In a grotesque attempt of turning adversity into opportunity, one manufacturer in China supplied face masks to Pakistan, made by converting bra cups into masks. Some others were more ingenious. When toilet paper ran out of super market shelves in Australia, tabloid NT News came to rescue of its readers by printing a special eight-page insert that can be cut and used as toilet paper!

India went into its first complete lockdown on 24th March, 2020, which resulted in closure of all manufacturing units, offices complexes, restaurants, malls and construction sites. State borders were closed, and airlines, trains, buses and local transport all came to a grinding halt.

Little did the policy makers think of migrant labourers from populated regions of the country who come to metro cities to earn their livelihood. Lockdown dealt a body blow to these migrant labourers. It was further compounded by fake reports of shortage of food and daily essentials, causing mass exodus of people. In absence of any available motorised transport, the desperate migrants embarked on a treacherous journey to their villages located as far as 1500 km on foot, with their belongings on head, and wife, elderly parents and small kids along. Local authorities had a tough time convincing people to go back to their homes while ensuring social distancing and providing for food and shelter for those who had reached a point of no return.

Some did reach their destination. But some reached the final one. In May, sixteen migrant labours from Aurangabad, while walking along railway tracks towards their hometown, were run over by a goods train. Hungry and tired, they sat on tracks to take a break from the arduous journey, only to soon fall asleep and never wakeup again.

Elsewhere in the world, wherever there are refugees and migrants struggling for survival, economic hardships due to COVID-19 have proven to be more fatal than the virus itself.

*Migrants returning home in India, after lockdown was announced on 24th March, 2020 ; Source: Google*

# CHAPTER FOUR

## THE CHINESE SOUP

"Waiter, There's a Rat in My Soup And it's Delicious" was the title of a story published in the Wall Street Journal, back in 1991. The story was about a restaurant owned by a former kitchen utensil salesman, Zhang Guoxun, in the Southern Chinese city of Guangzhou that specialized in rat-meat cuisine. The restaurant's menu was the brain child of Tang Qixin, a farmer honoured as a model worker by Mao Zedong in 1958 for his prowess as a rat killer in 1950's when Mao declared war on pests. The menu had thirty different rat dishes, including Liquored Rat Flambe, along with more mundane dishes such as Hot Pepper Silkworm, Raccoon With Winter Melon and Sliced Snake and Celery.

To put things in perspective, the Cantonese people of South China are legendary for eating anything that moves. The food markets here feature cats, raccoons, owls, doves and snakes along with bear and tiger's paw, dried deer penis and decomposed monkey skeletons. Eating wild animal or bush meat is considered a symbol of prosperity, as it is rare and expensive. Bush meat is considered more natural and nutritious compared to farmed meat. Extensive use of body parts of wild animals in traditional Chinese medicine for curing several ailments ranging from erectile dysfunction to rheumatoid arthritis, makes it even more attractive and sought after.

China is home to over 38,600 species of animals and plants, making it the third most bio-diverse country in the world after Brazil and Colombia. It is home to at least 590 species of mammals, 1288 species of birds and 490 species of reptiles and 461 species of amphibians. Such a biodiverse backyard, plush with wild species, indeed helps in promoting trade and consumption of wild animals.

The majority of viral outbreaks in recent history have emanated from China, caused by viruses of zoonotic origins. These viruses have crossed over from animals species to humans and have been traced to the "wet markets" of Southern China. The unsafe animal-human interaction in these markets is behind the spread of these zoonotic viruses to humans.

China was the ground zero for the most-deadly Severe Acute Respiratory Syndrome (SARS-CoV) outbreak in November 2002, also caused by a coronavirus. It spread to 37 countries, infecting 8,098 people and killing close 800 people over eight months.

In 2013, China reported the world's first-ever case of an avian influenza virus infecting humans. The H7N9 virus, which normally circulates among birds, was never found to have infected humans. Three years later, in 2016 too, a new strain of coronavirus was identified in China that killed 25,000 piglets, although it did not infect humans.

In 1993, Claude Hannoun, a leading expert from the Pasteur Institute in France, concluded that even in case of

1918 Spanish Flu, the precursor virus was likely to have originated in China. It then mutated in the United States near Boston, and from there, spread to Europe and rest of the world.

In his paper, *'Paths of Infection: The First World War and the Origins of the 1918 Influenza Epidemic'* published in January 2014 issue of the journal *War in History,* historian Dr Mark Humphries provides substantial documentary evidence to link a disease event in China in late 1917 and early 1918 to the Spanish Flu pandemic. His conclusion is based on archival evidence that a respiratory illness that struck northern China in November 1917 was identified a year later by Chinese health officials as identical to the Spanish flu. However, no tissue samples have survived for modern comparison. This illness was happening at the same time when the British were mobilizing 100,000 Chinese workers to work behind the British and French troops during the winter of 2017, shipping them across Canada in secret, sealed trains.

China was relatively less affected by the Spanish Flu. One of the reasons attributed to this phenomenon is the lower rates of flu mortality due to Chinese population's previously acquired immunity to the flu virus.

President Trump seems to have enough meat to feed on, and to justify his rhetoric of calling COVID-19 as 'The Chinese Virus' and most recently 'The Kung Flu.' These references angered the communist regime in China so much that they made it mandatory to register all clinical studies on the virus to be thoroughly scrutinized by the

Chinese authorities for any reference to virus origins before being published in clinical journals. Some call the reference to China as being racist. By the same logic, Spanish Flu, Middle East respiratory syndrome (MERS) and the super bug – New Delhi metallo-beta-lactamase 1(NDM-1) were all racist references. If the race is to save humanity, does the race of the virus really matter?

China is known for its opaque ways on most matters, and COVID-19 is no different. Whether it was suppressing initial news about the outbreak or hiding the actual number of casualties in the country, its actions raise suspicion. Some unverified reports suggest that the actual number of casualties in China were close to a whopping twelve million. Almost after a month of Wuhan being declared free from virus, China revised its reported death toll in Wuhan by 50% at 3,869 deaths, adding more teeth to global fury against its dubious handling of the crisis.

There were reports of legal suits being filed in US courts to sue China for causing and claiming reparations for the pandemic. One such suit was filed in Texas for $20 trillion by lawyer and right-wing activist Larry Klayman. He accused China of developing the virus in a laboratory with the aim to kill US citizens and entities in nations perceived to be an enemy of China. Anger against China was not limited to the US alone. Ministers in Japan and Brazil have also raised concerns over China's role in letting the virus spread to whole world to ensure its global supremacy.

Some voices on social media even demanded expulsion of China from the permanent membership of the UN

Security Council. Calls for boycott of China made products are already gaining steam in many countries.

China has also been accused of delaying the declaration of COVID-19 as a pandemic by the WHO. An early warning declaration by WHO could have potentially alarmed global community to gravity the impending threat. In March 2020, it vetoed a draft motion brought in UNSC by Estonia demanding 'complete transparency' on COVID-19 crisis with the help of Russia and South Africa.

China acted swiftly to change the global opinion. It promptly offered the gene sequence of the virus for vaccine discovery, made appeals to its Asian rivals like India, for not using the term Chinese Virus, and offered help to other countries in setting up makeshift hospitals and ensuring supply of ventilators and other essentials medical supplies.

Such was the desperation to salvage their tattered image that the Chinese Government went into an overdrive with their "wolf warrior diplomacy," soliciting letters of support and gratitude for Beijing's aid from government officials and the heads of major companies in Germany and Poland.

Clearly, China was more interested in saving face than saving lives.

To an extent, their efforts seemed to have borne fruit. The UNESCO came to its rescue and declared that the viruses have no nationality and that the fight against coronavirus needs science and not stigma. The state-owned Chinese media also played an important role. They launched a propaganda campaign to establish that COVID-19 actually spread out of the US and was carried to Wuhan by military delegates who attended the Military World Games held in Wuhan in October 2019.

As more and more people die of the pandemic – a quarter of them Americans – the war of words between US and China has got murkier with long term consequences for global geo-politics. The war against the pandemic is not likely to stay within hospitals and ICU wards. It will be intensely fought in diplomatic circles, international markets, newsrooms and on the web, fuelled and funded by state-backed media, military and opinion makers of both countries in months and probably, years to come.

After making frantic attempts to thwart any investigation into the source of origin of the virus, China finally succumbed to international pressure on 18th May, 2020 – a good four and a half months after the start of the crisis. At a virtual meeting of the World Health Assembly (WHA), the motion to launch a probe into origins of the virus was backed by more than 120 countries led by Europe and Australia. In bargain, China was successful in blocking entry of Taiwan to the WHA until the last quarter of the year, despite strong lobbying by the US in favour of its ally Taiwan.

Although the ruling communist party backed media attempt to package the WHA motion as an act of transparency by China, its heartburn on the matter was visible. It threatened to sanction individual US politicians who pushed for a legal action against China.

Punishing Australia, which was most vocal after US in demanding investigation into origins of the virus, China imposed 80.5 % duty on barley imports from Australia and called for a boycott of Australian products. After the motion was passed, China rubbished the Australian claim as a joke, and that its stand was vindicated by the WHA motion. Australia is world's most China-dependent developed economy, with nearly one third of its exports shipped to the country. Exports of agricultural produce, sale of international education and tourism to China are big revenue earners, while about half of its merchandise exports to China comprises iron ore.

China used the WHA event to woo a section of members who supported the motion by offering an aid of two billion dollars and helping thirty African countries by helping them strengthen their public health infrastructure.

This benevolence from China did little to bring about a change in President Trump's opinion of China. Towards end of May 2020, the Trump administration decided to cancel visas of thousands of Chinese graduate students and researchers in the United States who had direct ties to universities affiliated with the People's Liberation Army (PLA). A month later, The Pentagon released a list of twenty companies it believed are owned or controlled by PLA, suggesting likely US sanctions on them. The list included companies like Huawei Technologies, Aviation Industry Corporation of China, China Aerospace Science and Technology Corporation and China State Shipbuilding Corporation among several others. This move was in addition to the belligerent US stand on Hong Kong and Taiwan, which has furthered the divide between two largest global economies.

China has been the biggest beneficiary of globalisation, yet it has kept itself under wraps from the outer world, using its strict control over media and communication. The majority of the top 25 Chinese companies featured in the Fortune 500 list are owned by the Government. Even the private companies are not far from influence of the state, as most have business cells of the Communist Party of China (CPC). Almost all the listed Chinese internet firms have set up party committees and have senior executives who simultaneously serve as leaders of CPC. It was not until 2018, when in an innocuous mention in the CPC mouthpiece People's Daily, the world got to know that founders of three Chinese internet giants – Jack Ma of Alibaba, Baidu's Robin Li and Tencent's Pony Ma were all members of the CPC.

China's status as a manufacturing hub makes it difficult for countries, including the US, to immediately isolate China for its dubious ways. COVID-19 has, however, put China in a tight spot. It has lost trust of the global community. China is the leading global supplier of ventilators, hazmat suits, masks and other medical equipment needed to deal with the pandemic, one of the reasons many countries are not openly criticizing China. Once the pandemic is over, we may see a more vocal ostracization of China.

Some pundits are considering China's manufacturing sector as the biggest casualty of COVID-19. In the last thirty years, China emerged as the undisputed numero-uno in global manufacturing, controlling close to thirty percent of the global manufacturing output. It leads the world in production of steel, automotive components, medical equipment, mobile and computers, home appliances, active pharmaceuticals ingredients, specialty chemicals and toys, to name a few.

In a post COVID-19 world, coming to terms with the economic bloodbath and resultant job losses and unemployment, countries world over would be hard pressed to boost local industry and manufacturing. China stands to lose its sheen as a manufacturing powerhouse to countries such as India, Mexico, Vietnam, Bangladesh, Thailand, Cambodia and Indonesia.

Early signs are visible. Japan recently announced a trillion dollar recovery package to boost its bruised economy. Out of this, $ 2.2 billion was earmarked to help firms in shifting production back to Japan and $ 200 million earmarked for firms seeking to move manufacturing base to other countries. Such an action by a friendly country in the neighbourhood could trigger a larger flight of companies from China.

Alarmed with Bank of China increasing its stake to 1% in its largest private sector bank HDFC, Indian Government swiftly changed its FDI rules to prohibit Chinese investors taking advantage of the slump in economy to takeover Indian companies. Italy, Spain and Germany have already tightened their FDI rules to limit Chinese stakes. The move was triggered after China reportedly acquired stakes in 30% European companies in bargain deals post

*FDI - Foreign Direct Investment*

COVID 19. Virtual world behemoths from China, Zoom and TikTok, are already under the scanner in many countries due to privacy and data safety issues. India banned fifty-nine Chinese apps in late June on account of data safety concerns. Such has been the scepticism over China that the United Nations, which had roped in Chinese company, Tencent, for its 75th Anniversary celebrations, had to dump the deal after concerns were raised over its track record on transparency.

Chinese internet giant, Huawei, has been at the receiving end of prevailing global mistrust against China. It is the world's largest providers of telecommunications equipment, networking gear and smartphones. Aligning themselves with the US concerns on security, many countries are having second thoughts on using Huawei services, as the race to upgrade telecom infrastructure to 5G begins worldwide. US, Australia, UK, Singapore, Sweden, Denmark, the Czech Republic, Poland, Estonia, Romania, Latvia and Greece are already part of the club. Germany and France are likely to follow suit.

The US and China were already engaged in an trade war before COVID-19 happened, which has further deepened with US openly accusing China of letting the virus cross its border and making the world pay for it. The US considers itself the biggest victim of the 'Kung Flu.' This pandemic has exposed fault lines of the US healthcare system, famed intelligence machinery and disregard for international organisation like the WHO. President Trump, who may find it difficult to make a comeback post the elections scheduled during the year end, would leave no stone unturned to turn tables on China for spreading the virus in the US and elsewhere. To divert attention from lacuna of his own leadership and mismanagement of the pandemic, it would not be limited to mere rhetoric, but also become accentuated in form of steps to curb its business exposure to China. It may culminate into a full blown standoff on many fronts, military included.

China is not sitting idle either. It has resorted to taking aggressive positions in the South China Sea and its borders with India. One of the objectives is to engage its potential economic rivals in conflicts, and distract them from economic reforms which may eventually snatch manufacturing away from China. On 15th June, 2020, one such incident of transgression on the Indian border in Ladakh, took a bloody turn, claiming the lives of 20 soldiers on the Indian side and double the numbers on the Chinese side. As the eye ball to eye ball confrontation between the two countries continued, US called for re-deployment of its military, alluding to the South China Sea region. US lawmaker Ted Yoho even called for global coalition to tackle China expansionist tendencies. Flexing its muscles, in early July, the US deployed two of its aircraft carriers – the first-in-class USS Nimitz and the USS Ronald Reagan in the South China Sea.

China has effectively used its debt-trap diplomacy in lesser developed economies of Asia and Africa to keep things in its favour at international forums. In Africa, from 2010 to 2016, Chinese debt burden has increased from $ 10 billion to $ 30 billion, with countries reeling under the heavy load of debt from China slowly realizing the hidden agenda.

A case in point is Tonga. From 2013 to 2014, the country suffered a debt crisis, claiming 44% of Tonga's GDP. The top five countries in Africa with the largest current Chinese debt are Angola ($25 billion), Ethiopia ($13.5 billion), Kenya ($7.9 billion), the Republic of Congo ($7.3 billion) and North Sudan ($6.4 billion). Another victim of the Chinese debt trap is Sri Lanka, where it had to lease out the Hambantota Port to China, which it built with borrowed funds from EXIM bank of China. Built with doubtful commercial logic, Hambantota Port is critical due to its strategic importance to China. Its Belt and Road initiative has already caused some strains in otherwise-rock-solid nexus with neighbouring Pakistan.

The unpleasant trade war, the ongoing bickering over the virus origin with US, its antagonizing "wolf warrior diplomacy," acts of transgressions in South China Sea and nefarious actions on its border with India would only complicate matters for China, making it a global pariah in the long term.

China running out of favour seems to be flavour of the soup, we all are in at the moment.

# CHAPTER FIVE

## FAILING THE LITMUS TEST

Public health events that endanger international public health are determined under the International Health Regulations (2005). Such events are classified as a Public Health Emergency of International Concern (PHEIC, pronounced, incredibly, "fake!"). The declaration of a PHEIC serves as a clarion call to the international community to provide political, financial and technical support to a public health emergency. Responsibility of determining whether an event can be termed PHEIC, lies with the WHO Director-General, and requires the convening of a committee of experts – the Emergency Committee. At least one member of the Emergency Committee should be an expert nominated by the State within whose territory the event arises. In this case, it had to be China.

The very first meeting of WHO Emergency Committee (EC) on the virus outbreak in Wuhan, was held on 22nd and 23rd January, 2020 in Geneva via teleconference, with the aim to decide and advice WHO Director General, Dr Tedros Adhanom Ghebreyesus on declaring the outbreak, a PHEIC. By then, close to 560 cases and 17 deaths had already been reported from China, mostly from Wuhan, and some even outside Hubei province. Cases were also registered in Thailand, South Korea, Singapore and Japan.

The committee chaired by Professor Didier Houssin, a French professor of surgery and a liver transplant specialist, decided that it was too early to declare a PHEIC. It acknowledged the severity of the infection and the potential for human-to-human transmission.

It is important to note that the EC had divergent views on this. Unable to reach a conclusion, EC held a vote, which ended in a tie. A tie had happened for the first time in history of EC! Who scored in the tie breaker round remains a mystery. More bizarre is the cause of divergence between the EC members, which centred on the meaning of 'international spread.' Since at the time of meeting, only four cases were reported outside China, all with travel history to China, it was decided that such cases did not constitute 'international spread' and hence, PHEIC is not required.

However, as per WHO constitution, for a disease to be declared a PHEIC, it must constitute a public health risk to other States through the international spread of disease, and it potentially requires a coordinated international response. That is, it must merely have the potential or potential risk of cross-border transmission. On a similar premise, the resurgent wild Polio was declared a PHEIC without having cross-border transmission in 2014. In that case, risk of international spread was the determining factor. The exporting states then were Afghanistan, Cameroon, Equatorial Guinea, Ethiopia, Israel, Nigeria, Pakistan, Somalia and the Syrian Arab Republic. The head of WHO then was a Chinese-Canadian Dr Margaret Chan, while Dr Tedros was serving as the Foreign Minister of Ethiopia.

By 25th January, 2020, multiple cases had already been confirmed and reported from Australia, Canada, Thailand, Korea, Singapore, Japan, Malaysia, Ivory Coast, USA, Taiwan, Hong Kong, Macau and Vietnam.

The WHO declared corona virus outbreak, a PHEIC on 30th January, 2020, albeit with no travel and trade restriction advisory. The virus had already spread to 19 countries, with close to 8000 confirmed cases, and had consumed 170 lives till then.

*Bureaucrazy* be damned!

On 11th March, 2020, COVID-19 was finally declared a Pandemic by the WHO. That was after more than two months since the first case of the novel corona virus was reported to the WHO. At that time, the virus had consumed 4,600 people and affected close to 135,000 people in 118 countries.

As the crisis unfolded, WHO Chief Dr Tedros's initial handling of the crisis was being increasingly questioned. An online petition on *change.org* platform, calling for his resignation as WHO Chief had gained close to 750,000 signatures worldwide by end March 2020, accusing him of underestimating the situation and being soft on China.

In mid-January, when China refused WHO's request to send a team of scientific observers to Wuhan, Dr Tedros chose to ignore the snub. He went on to praise Chinese efforts in containing the outbreak, despite being aware of China's complicity in suppressing information about the outbreak. Even after declaring the PHEIC, he advocated against travel and trade restrictions. Such is his camaraderie with China that every allegation on China gets an immediate rebuttal from WHO. When China revised its death toll in Wuhan by 50%, WHO came to its rescue, arguing that this is a normal practice, as countries would keep revising the numbers.

The reasons for his bonhomie with China are not unfounded. Dr Tedros was elected as WHO director general in July 2017 with the support of a bloc of Asian and African countries. Chinese diplomats were pivotal in mobilizing support for Dr Tedros, using Chinese influence among the African union and Asian countries. As per reports, when Dr Tedros was the foreign minister of Ethiopia, Chinese investments in the country rose significantly. One of the first few countries he visited soon after his election to WHO was China, where he was quite generous in his praise of the healthcare system. WHO's role in ignoring the alarm raised by Taiwan as early as December 2019 about human to human transmission of the virus and his own allegations of racism, accusing Taiwan, only indicates his allegiance to China.

President Trump shocked the world on 29th May, 2020, by announcing his decision to sever all ties with WHO, citing its role in handling the pandemic, connivance with China and its reluctance to carry out structural reforms. Following footsteps of his ideological ally, President Bolsonaro of Brazil too threatened to quit the WHO dubbing it a "partisan political organization." Frustration of other nations was equally visible. Japan's Deputy Prime Minister and Finance Minister Taro Aso, upset with an estimated loss of $14 Billion on account of postponement of Tokyo Olympics, went to extent of calling the WHO as "Chinese Health Organization."

Dr Tedros was elected to WHO in the first ever secret ballot election, where all members had a vote. He is the first African and the first non-physician to be elected to the top job at WHO. As health minister of Ethiopia, he is credited with reforming the country's health system. During his seven years at the helm, Ethiopia built thousands of new health centres in rural areas and introduced health insurance system. The mortality rate from diseases like tuberculosis, malaria and AIDS fell sharply, while the number of medical schools increased ten times from a paltry three.

Despite his several achievements, Dr Tedros is not new to controversies. His election to the WHO was mired with allegations of covering up several outbreaks of cholera in Ethiopia between 2006 and 2011 as 'watery diarrhoea,' even though clinical evidence suggested it was cholera. His being part of an authoritarian regime in Ethiopia that persecuted members of the opposition and journalists, further add to his controversial charisma.

In one of his most controversial decisions, soon after taking over as WHO Director General, was the appointment of Zimbabwean dictator, Robert Mugabe, as a goodwill ambassador for non-communicable diseases. Given Mugabe's track record on human rights abuse, his appointment created a global furore, forcing Dr Tedros to rescind the appointment. Many believe the appointment was a quid-pro-quo for the support of African Union during his election to the WHO, which was then headed by Mugabe. His role in the fiasco earned him the sobriquet of 'Dictator General' by *The Lancet,* a prominent medical journal.

Dr Tedros has adopted an unconventional approach in leading the WHO, which has mostly been headed by career diplomats influenced by the West. Be it visiting the epidemic affected regions himself, appointing a lesser known Russian official Dr Tereza Kasaeva as Head of Global TB programme, or appointment of several women as WHO Regional Directors, his moves have been unconventional. His efforts to change the status quo in functioning of WHO and making it more diverse and decentralized seems to be reflected in his dealing with the current pandemic as well.

One of the reasons attributed for the mismanagement of Ebola outbreak in West Africa in 2014 was the lack of coordination between the WHO headquarters and its regional offices in Africa. The disaster was so grave that the US and several other nations had to deploy more than 5,000 troops at the request of affected countries, and an ad-hoc UN committee was created to take over responsibilities from the WHO. Dr Tedros's initial reliance on the Chinese version about the virus outbreak and praise for its handling of the pandemic appears to be a cautionary approach in which he wanted to avoid a similar mistake by his predecessor, Dr Margaret Chan.

As a seven-year-old, Dr Tedros had witnessed the death of his three-year old young brother who succumbed to measles due to lack of proper health care system in Ethiopia. In his own words, this early incident in his life drove him to work towards improving health care systems across the world.

Even before the election of Dr Tedros, WHO was losing its clout. In an increasingly nationalistic world, with nations under control of head strong and some eccentric leaders, its job of driving healthcare initiatives in 194 member countries has become even more complex. In absence of any power to impose stringent measures on member states, it has to work its way through soft dealing, which, in times of emergencies, is mostly inefficient. A major challenge lies in the source of its funding. Only 20% of the WHO expenditure comprises of compulsory contributions by member states, the rest comes from voluntary contributions from States and NGOs such as the Bill and Melinda Gates Foundation, which is the single largest private donor to WHO.

On the same day when Dr Tedros was elected, US announced cuts to funding of various global health initiatives. It eventually withdrew its $400 million contribution to the global health agency. This may trigger a rethink on funds flowing in from other donor countries like the UK, Germany and France, paving the way for China to increase its clout in the WHO.

The WHO has a pivotal role in the current pandemic and beyond. It's an organisation too big to fail. In the past, WHO has been successful in eradicating small pox, restricting polio to only three countries and in controlling the spread of HIV and SARS pandemics. It was successful in doing so despite having a structure, which at the best, is limited to issuing advisory and coordination among countries. It does not have sweeping powers like the WTO or the UN Security Council. The key reason for its success in the past were the individuals who withstood manipulation and bullying by powerful member countries.

A case in point is Dr Gro Harlem Brundtland, who was the Director General of WHO during the SARS outbreak in 2003. She was swift in condemning China for not reporting the outbreak in time and also issued advisory against travelling to affected countries like China, Hong Kong, Vietnam and Canada. Then, WHO's response to SARS was a major success, with less than 1,000 deaths and limited spread to twenty-six countries. Due to the WHO's proactive efforts, the SARS pandemic was defeated without vaccines or medicines. Non-pharmaceutical interventions led by WHO, such as travel warnings, tracking, testing, isolating cases and information-gathering were the key success factors. All this was made possible by the efforts of then WHO chief. It might be already too late for Dr Tedros to take the cue, though.

As WHO chief, presiding over the global efforts to contain the pandemic, Dr Tedros has become a house-hold name worldwide. His place in history hinges on the fate of the pandemic. Untill then, we need to have faith in his efforts and wish they bear fruit.

In one of his early speeches, Dr Tedros promised to shake up the WHO. He meant it literally; the audience would know now!

# CHAPTER SIX

## THE MOMENT OF RECKONING

Donald Henry Rumsfeld served as the US Secretary of Defence from 1975 to 1977 and from 2001 to 2006. As Secretary of Defence, Rumsfeld's claims that Iraq had weapons of mass destruction (WMDs) led to the invasion of Iraq, although the much-hyped stockpiles of nuclear and biological weapons were never found. Billions of American taxpayer's money was spent in destroying a country based on misplaced hype and scare about the non-existent WMDs.

During the intervening period from 1977 to 2001, he served on boards of several private companies. Prior to joining the Bush administration in 2001, his last assignment was with Gilead Sciences Inc. He joined Gilead as a director in 1988 and was appointed chairman in 1997, succeeding its founder-chairman, Michael L. Riordan, who founded Gilead in 1987. Donald Rumsfeld held a stake in Gilead estimated to be worth $5-$25 million in 2004.

Scientists at Gilead Sciences invented the drug Tamiflu by synthesizing *shikimic* acid, an extract of the spice herb, star anise. Gilead licensed their relevant patents to Roche in 1996. It was later approved as a first in class drug in US and Europe in 1999 and 2002, respectively, for the treatment of influenza.

Tamiflu had a lacklustre start. Gilead, which was entitled to royalty payments on sales of Tamiflu was bickering with Roche over the ongoing neglect of the product, and had even threatened to terminate the exclusive agreement for sales and marketing of the drug.

Voila! Here comes the bird flu.

In January 2005, news of an outbreak of Avian influenza in Vietnam spread like wild fire across the world. Up to 140 million birds died or were forcefully killed due to the scare of an outbreak. The outbreak did spread to several Asian countries, the Russian region, North Africa and Middle East. In September 2005, David Nabarro, then Senior United Nations System Coordinator for Avian and Human Influenza, warned the world that an outbreak of avian influenza could kill up to 150 million people. The Infectious Disease Society of America (IDSA) advocated expanding the national stockpile of anti-viral drug, Tamiflu, to at least a quarter of the population.

The threat of an impending pandemic created global demand for Tamiflu, causing worldwide shortages of the drug. In a stockpiling frenzy, US ended up stockpiling more than $1 billion worth of the drug. In 2005, Tamiflu sales zoomed 400% clocking $2 billion in global revenues. Gilead's share price rose by more than three times, earning a fortune for the illustrious Mr Rumsfeld.

In wake of the worldwide Swine Flu pandemic, Tamiflu was added to the WHO's list of essential medications in 2010. Close to a hundred countries had built Tamiflu stocks to cover an estimated 350 million people. Tamiflu generated total sales in excess of $18 billion since its launch in 1999. Half of it is attributed to stockpiling frenzy by various governments based on fears of a pandemic which started with Avian Flu and peaked during the Swine Flu outbreak in April 2009.

Fortunately, between 2003- 2019, global death toll, as reported by WHO, due to the Avian flu, was less than 500.

One of the major reasons for massive stockpiling of Tamiflu were the claims by drug maker, Roche, that it reduces hospitalizations and serious complications of flu. In 2014, Cochrane, a voluntary collaboration of 30,000 scientific experts from around the world, published a report claiming that the original evidence presented by Roche to government agencies around the world was incomplete, raising questions about the accuracy of these claims and the efficacy of Tamiflu. A majority of these clinical trials were funded by Roche, which marketed and promoted the drug. It acknowledged the minor benefits on symptom relief, such as shortening duration of symptoms by half a day on average, but concluded that there was little evidence to support that use of Tamiflu reduced hospitalization, or the risk of developing confirmed pneumonia, or it prevented person-to-person spread of influenza. In addition, there were reports of "abnormal behaviour" and a few deaths after Tamiflu intake in Japan, once the biggest consumer of Tamiflu in the world, which forced Roche to revise the drug label to add potential psychiatric events as side effects of the drug.

Tamiflu patents started expiring in 2016. After being on the WHO list of essential medicines for seven years, it was downgraded to "complementary" status in 2017. Availability of cheaper versions of the drug has led to annual global sales dwindling to under $500 million.

In January 2020, Dr Tom Jefferson, a British epidemiologist and lead author of the Cochrane report, sued Roche under the US False Claims Act for making unsubstantiated claims that Tamiflu could significantly mitigate the risk of a flu pandemic, thereby defrauding federal and state governments of $1.5 billion. If the lawsuit is successful, Jefferson gets one third of any recoveries made. A win-win for all!

The Tamiflu saga is just one of the many skeletons which keep tumbling out of the pharmaceutical industry, highlighting nexus of politicians, lobbyists, key opinion makers, drug regulators and 'Big Pharma,' and how they manipulate the system and human behaviour for their own vested interests. In the US alone, the industry has spent close to $4.45 billion over the past twenty-two years in lobbying for their causes which ranges from making a case for faster drug approval process for new drugs, patent regime, funding of research programs to resisting reduction in drug prices. Pharmaceutical industry is by far the largest spender on lobbying in the US and notoriously comprises key opinion leaders and influencers with access into the alleys of power. As on March 2020, 63% of these lobbyists were former US government employees.

The drug pricing scandal involving *Turing Pharmaceuticals* is still fresh in public memory as one the most avaricious attempts to exploit patient suffering for windfall gains by any pharmaceutical company. In 2015, price of an off-patent drug, Daraprim – an anti-parasitic medication used to treat AIDS patients was increased overnight from $13.50 to $750 per pill, an increase of over 5000%. In absence of any generics, patients had no substitutes for the drug.

Following demand for investigation by Senator Bernie Sanders into its pricing practices, the company initially agreed to reduce the price by 50%, which was later retracted. The company had hired four lobbyists from *Buchanan, Ingersoll & Rooney* with backgrounds in health care legislation and pharmaceutical pricing and a Washington based PR firm, DCI group, to tide over the public fury. Despite the public outrage, its price has not been reduced, although a generic version of the drug was approved recently in February 2020.

Even the approaching pandemic failed to rein in the temptation for a few. As soon as the threat from COVID-19 became apparent, US firm *Rising Pharmaceuticals* doubled the price of chloroquine (an antimalarial, which was being tested for COVID-19) on 23rd January, 2020. Later, the public backlash led them to retract the unethical price increase.

Terrorists and dictators are not always the only one spreading terror and suffering!

The global pharmaceutical industry is worth $1.3 trillion. More than 70% drug revenues come from the US, Europe and Japan. Two thirds of it comes from US alone, making it primo-uomo of the pharmaceutical industry. Higher drug prices, evolved insurance and reimbursement systems and advanced healthcare infrastructure make these markets attractive for Big Pharma. It is only logical for them to prioritize drug development for diseases with higher prevalence or incidence in these markets. Unfortunately, 70% of the world population resides elsewhere and is relatively less privileged. Public health priorities of a large portion of world population and commercial interests of Big Pharma do not match. This is a fundamental flaw in the modus operandi of an industry whose primary purpose is to alleviate human suffering, irrespective of how deep the patients' pockets are.

Pandemics are unpredictable. They may or may not last long enough or reoccur to create a market opportunity big enough to justify huge investments in research and development for vaccines and drugs to treat them. The high risk-high reward business model does not work well in case of pandemics. The market opportunity dries up as soon as the crisis ends, leading to freeze in funding and closure of R&D projects.

GSK's experience in Ebola is one such example. It invested for years in three vaccine candidates. In the final stage of clinical trials, the projects were shelved due to a dwindling number of Ebola cases towards the end of epidemic. With no real prospect of a financial return, it handed over the candidates to a non-profit institute in the US. Ebola cases have resurfaced recently, soon after the Democratic Republic of the Congo declared itself - "Ebola Free".

Vaccine development is a difficult, expensive and time-consuming process with no guarantee of returns. The last "blockbuster vaccine" produced in the private sector was Merck's HPV* vaccine, Gardasil, which was launched in 2006 after a 20-year investment in R&D.

Vaccines are the least preferred, as they provide immunity from a certain ailment, blocking future revenue streams. Viral epidemics such as SARS, Swine Flu, MERS, Zika and Ebola have consumed more than half a billion people in last eighteen years. Yet, despite clear indications that another viral pandemic could emerge, Big Pharma has not shown proactive interest to develop effective vaccines or medicines which can help in avoiding and controlling these virus outbreaks.

Take the case of Ebola. The virus was first identified in 1976. Vaccine development first began in the late 1970s. Since the outbreaks were rare and had been controlled quickly, there was little interest shown by pharmaceuticals companies in advance stage development. It was only fast-tracked after the West Africa outbreak and WHO declaring it a 'global health emergency' in August 2014. The vaccine approved last year in US and Europe was developed by a government lab in Canada, which was later picked up by Merck, quoting 'moral clarity' that they should to do something on the

*HPV : Human Papillomavirus

outbreak. The realization only happened after the Canadian government donated the vaccine candidate to WHO and the virus threatened the developed world.

The latest Access to Medicines Index 2020, which analyses R&D projects of the twenty biggest pharmaceutical companies, reveals none of them prioritizes projects on vaccines or treatments for SARS, MERS, Zika or Ebola. It would be interesting to see if COVID-19 can bring about a change in their priorities. Commercially, less lucrative vaccines business model has led to the exit of major players. Novartis sold its vaccine division to GSK in 2014 after operating at a loss for years. Business consolidation has left only four major players, controlling 80% of the nearly $45 billion market.

One important factor is that pandemics predominantly affect the less privileged, and often originate in underdeveloped or developing economies. The same is true even for acute ailments which require medication for limited duration, tropical and neglected diseases. Big Pharma has stopped investing in new antibiotics to treat drug-resistant infections, which is one of the biggest health crises of our times. While new drug development for lifestyle ailments like Diabetes or CNS disorders, which require long term or lifelong medication, has long been a focus of Big Pharma, patent expiries and generic availability have led them to shift focus on costly cancer treatments and orphan indications which provide tax incentives and longer market exclusivity.

Another argument, although seemingly outrageous, explains the reluctance of Big Pharma in developing medications which completely cure ailments. It is pretty simple; they don't want to develop medications which are 100% effective since it is not a sustainable model. To bolster the argument, they cite the example of novel hepatitis C drugs - Sovaldi and Harvoni launched by Gilead in 2013 and 2014 respectively. Their introduction was an overwhelming success, as they provided more than 90% cure rate for hepatitis C in 12 weeks of treatment. The near cure, gradually exhausted the available pool of treatable patients. Being a transmittable infectious disease, curing existing patients also decreased the number of carriers able to transmit the virus to new patients, which led to a decline in addition of new patient pool and reducing the addressable market opportunity. Sales revenue of both drugs, which peaked to $19 billion in 2015, have since declined to early single digit billions.

In 2017, an EU proposal to fast-track vaccine development for viral diseases to ensure availability before an outbreak was rejected by Big Pharma. A similar proposal mooted by The Coalition of Epidemic Preparedness Innovations (CEPI) foundation based in Washington DC also failed to gain traction.

Pandemics do provide an opportunity for Big Pharma to generate opportunistic revenues. The global scare and scale caused by the pandemic, besides offering large revenue upsides, also offers early entry to the market and relaxation in regulatory and clinical requirements – significant privileges in a highly regulated world of pharmaceuticals.

Regulators tend to be relatively lenient on otherwise-stringent parameters during pandemics. Those were possibly the underlying reasons for Tamiflu's dream run during the Avian Flu hoax and Swine Flu pandemic. The 'saviour of humanity' tag which comes along, is an icing on the cake. It adds the much-needed image boost to an industry, which is often at the receiving end of public scrutiny.

The positive news about scientists racing against time to develop a COVID-19 vaccine, extensive media coverage of even a marginal efficacy of an existing drug, or a minor breakthrough in drug development status, helps in building a narrative that Big Pharma is responding like never before to the current catastrophe.

In a public relation overdrive, Johnson & Johnson (J&J), which has been facing numerous lawsuits for its role in the opioid crisis in the US and cancer-causing baby talc, launched an eight episode series titled "The Road to a Vaccine." The series hosted by award-winning journalist Lisa Ling features guests from medical community, and takes viewers through the vaccine development process. It went on air in mid-April, each 30-minute episode went live online on Tuesdays on Facebook, Twitter, LinkedIn and J&J website.

Caught unprepared for the current pandemic, Big Pharma is trying to dig gold in a garbage dump. Decades-old drugs are being re-purposed to treat patients infected with the virus. Drug regulators too have obliged by approving them for emergency use, even in absence of long term safety and efficacy data. The USFDA approved

Hydroxychloroquine for emergency use on 25th March ,2020, only to revoke the approval three months later, based on adverse clinical findings. Anti-viral combination Lopinavir / Ritonavir was used effectively in South Korea, but later trials found it to be ineffective. Favipiravir was approved in Japan, China and India for its efficacy in reducing the viral load. In early July, WHO abandoned the clinical trial arms of the Solidarity Trial being conducted with Hydroxychloroquine and Lopinavir / Ritonavir as they failed to reduce the mortality rate in hospitalized patients of COVID-19. Doctors in Bangladesh have touted a combination of the lice killer Ivermectin and antibiotic Doxycycline as a potential therapy yielding "astounding results." In a promising breakthrough, WHO announced the effectiveness of Dexamethasone in reducing mortality rates among critically-ill patients.

The current enthusiasm to qualify drugs even with marginal utility in treating COVID-19 patients is akin to the one witnessed during the Spanish flu. Aspirin lost its patent in February 1917, prompting many manufacturers into the lucrative Aspirin market. During the 1918 flu, doctors, then unaware of the toxic side effects of Asprin, used to prescribe the drug in frequent high doses, causing pulmonary edema, which contributed to overall higher mortality during the pandemic. The toxicity level of Aspirin in high doses was not known until 1960s. It was only in 1977, when the US drug regulator issued dose recommendation for Aspirin, cautioning about the risks with higher-than-prescribed limits and dosing frequency.

*Source: New-York Tribune, 14<sup>th</sup> April, 1918*

Some have indeed dug gold in the scavenging spree. Gilead is testing Remdesivir, an anti-viral originally developed in 2009, for hepatitis C. It failed to deliver the desired results against hepatitis C. Later, it was repurposed as a potential treatment for Ebola virus disease, but was found ineffective. It was subsequently discovered that the drug had antiviral activity against multiple viruses, including coronaviruses responsible for SARS and MERS.

Despite potential side effects, the drug has gained authorization for emergency use in the US, UK, India, Singapore, Europe and Japan. It's under investigation as part of the Solidarity Trials being conducted under the aegis of WHO. In absence of any effective alternative, it remains the poster boy among several other drug candidates under evaluation for COVID-19.

More than forty vaccine candidates are in various stages of clinical development; a majority of them are in pre-clinical or early research phase. Seven of them are in late stage clinical development. Chances of a successful vaccine candidate being available are only fifty percent. If successful, the earliest vaccine candidate will not be hit the market before mid-2021 for mass administration. Even then, issues related to price, access and availability remain to be resolved. Once the vaccine is available, 60-70% people need to be vaccinated in order to stop the spread, which is known as herd immunity. Still, that would mean billions of people around the world!

Daily updates on the status of vaccines and drugs under development or being approved in some or the other part of the world have raised our hopes for a breakthrough in resolving the COVID-19 juggernaut. It's a moving target. When will this wild virus chase end? No one has a clue.

Enough has been said about the unscrupulous practices and priorities of Big Pharma. The pharmaceutical industry is just part of the larger system which has evolved over years as an outcome of the evils engrained in human nature. Inherent human emotion of avarice and insecurity have become a corporate practice, as some individuals gain the power to pass it off as a reflection of collective conscience.

This pandemic gave us a peek into this transition as well. Driven by President Trump's 'America First' rhetoric, the US administration tried to secure exclusive rights of a promising COVID-19 vaccine from a German biotech firm – CureVac. This gluttonous behaviour was again at display when he secured all Gilead stocks of Remdesivir to be manufactured till September for US, leaving other countries to fend for themselves. Neither this is the first time, nor is he the only one resorting to such behaviour. During the Ebola outbreak in 2014, an experimental therapy called Zmapp was making headlines. Still an experimental drug then, a mass scramble followed. High income countries, US and Spain, procured Zmapp for their health workers, while doctors and nurses in West Africa were largely left without an effective treatment. Similar behaviour was seen among the European nations. France, Germany, Italy and the Netherlands struck a deal with drug maker, AstraZeneca, for its vaccine candidate, offering others to join the alliance on similar terms. Whether poor countries could afford those terms, is a different question.

When the virus was engulfing the entire world, creating panic, images of people hoarding toilet paper across US, EU and Australia left us wondering, '*What made them poop so much?* ' It was nothing but blatant greed disguised as panic. Be it poop or pill, greed just made another kill!

This pandemic provides the much-needed pause for Big Pharma, policy makers and individuals who drive decisions at these organizations to strike the right balance of profits, patient welfare and priorities in drug development. It's time to shun selfish, unitary goals and adopt an industry model that is driven by public interest and rewards treatments which alleviate the suffering of larger humanity, and not just a few with deep pockets. Vaccines, infectious diseases, tropical diseases and neglected diseases should get equal priority and focus in Big Pharma board rooms, as a cancer or diabetes drug would get.

Small steps make a large impact. One man's vision and desire to reduce human suffering brought a new ray of hope for HIV patients worldwide. It was a profit-oriented generic pharmaceutical company in India – Cipla, which decided to make treatments available at a fractional cost, lifting the death sentence for millions across the developing world. *"None shall be denied"* should be the motto of all pharmaceuticals companies around the world.

*"None shall be denied" is the official motto of CIPLA*

It is now turn of Big Pharma to drive this transformation. An encouraging start was made by Abbvie by deliberately letting go of the Orphan drug status; it was granted for its anti-viral drug Kaletra (Lopinavir/Ritonavir) for treating COVID-19 patients. The orphan drug status would have entitled the drug to command high prices, huge tax breaks and longer market exclusivity, enabling them to keep away lower-priced generics but restricting access to several needy patients.

Gilead too followed suit by rescinding the orphan drug status for its drug, Remdesivir. It has walked the extra mile by giving voluntary license to generic manufacturers in India and Pakistan to make cost-effective versions of the drug, increasing its access to the less-privileged patients in developing countries.

It would be grossly indecorous to ignore the contribution of Big Pharma and myriad other pharmaceutical companies in providing treatment options for a wide range of ailments. It is impossible to imagine a world without GSK's Augmentin or Bayer's Aspirin. Hopes remain high until we have a Pfizer and its Viagra!

COVID-19 pandemic is a moment for Big Pharma and larger pharmaceutical industry to return to its primary purpose of alleviating human suffering, which has been overpowered by obscene pricing, unethical marketing practice and exaggerated claims.

The moment of reckoning for the industry is here. It's now or never.

# CHAPTER SEVEN

## SACRED VERSES

Religion, per se, has never been a saviour of humanity. On the contrary, it has only perpetrated hatred, inequality and ignorance. COVID-19 once again exposes the sham we all follow in name of religion. Iconic structures of the Vatican and the Mecca, umpteen Hindu Shrines and Buddhist Monasteries have all turned into mere tokens of collective human ego, standing helpless to the believers and non-believers alike.

Blind faith in religion blended with ignorance and dash of arrogance works to the advantage of the deadly virus. Stronger the blend, the harder it becomes to reason with believers, making it difficult to implement measures necessary to contain the virus from spreading further. In South Asian countries of India, Pakistan and Bangladesh, such believers were found in abundance during the pandemic. The fight here was not with the virus alone. In Bangladesh, thousands of people in the port city of Chittagong defied the nationwide lockdown to mourn the death of a cleric, whereas Pakistan officially declared opening of mosques, and allowed gathering during the month of Ramadhan.

Such acts of blasphemous logic are not restricted to any particular religion. Cow urine suddenly became the elixir of immortality for some religious enthusiasts in India, while in Myanmar, a prominent Buddhist monk announced that a dose of one lime and three palm seeds would confer immunity from the virus. In Iran, a few pilgrims attempted eternity by licking Shite Muslim shrines to ward off infection. And in Texas USA, a Christian preacher braided televangelism and telemedicine with his one hand outstretched, as he claimed to cure believers right through their screens!

Several religious festivals like Navratri, Good Friday and the holy month of Ramadhan coincided, while COVID-19 graph was shooting upwards in most parts of the world. Ramadan is the holiest month for close to two billion Muslims all over the world, during which they fast in daylight hours, congregate for prayers and share meals as a community. During Ramadhan, Muslims wake up early to eat a pre-dawn meal called Suhoor or Sehri, and break their fast after sunset with a meal called Iftaar. Breaking of the fast is usually a social affair with people organising Iftaar dinners for friends and family, or community meals for the less privileged. Mosques host large Iftaars, especially for the poor.

The pandemic ruined Ramadhan festivities for most Muslims across the globe. Countries had to advise its citizens to avoid large prayer gatherings and have Sehri and Iftaars individually or with family at home. In Iran, among the first and the worst-hit Muslim countries, its Supreme Leader Ayatollah Ali Khamenei called on people to avoid collective prayers. In Saudi Arabia, King Salman ordered the shortening of Tarawih prayers, which were held without public attendance at the two holy mosques in Mecca and Medina. In Malaysia, all religious gatherings were banned until 31st May, 2020. Jordan suspended the special evening Tarawih prayers at mosques, urging citizens to offer them at home.

Jerusalem's Al-Aqsa Mosque compound remained closed for prayers, although the prayer calls still took place five times a day. In the UK, mosques held online sermons and virtual prayers sessions. Pakistan allowed mosques to remain open for prayers during Ramadhan, albeit with social distancing guidelines.

Shia shrines in Iraq, Iran and Mecca in Saudi Arabia were closed even before the holy month of Ramadhan started on 24th April, 2020. In normal times, these shrines would draw millions of pilgrims throughout the year, with people coming in close contact with each other. These religious sites are prone to spreading infections, as Muslims kiss the walls of these shrines, making them high risk zones for spreading the virus.

The restrictions imposed were mandatory and very much needed to contain the spread of virus further. However, not many felt the same. Special burial restrictions and protocols were questioned by many, fanning protests in Iran and Morocco, pushing the Government to get Fatwas issued, making it a mandatory religious practice.

Such restrictions were considered an attack on religious freedom and repression of minority rights, especially in countries where Muslims are not a majority. In India, which is home to the second largest Muslim population in the world, some felt these restrictions were an act of oppression. Such apprehensions were also fuelled by a section of media, trying to give a religious hue to an act of irresponsible behaviour by a few. The Tablighi Jamaat event in Delhi, believed to be a major reason behind the spurt in cases in India, was reported in such a shamefully biased manner that it maligned the entire Muslim community as 'corona carriers.'

Muslim vendors were shunned by many, based on rumours of them spitting on fruits and vegetables they sell. Some stopped eating Halal meat usually sold only by Muslims. Such events gave ammunition to vested interests to propagate their own political agenda. Pakistan launched a campaign using the event to portray the image of India as an oppressor of Muslim minority rights, especially via diplomatic channels, social media and lobby groups in US, EU and Middle East. Later, many of the social media links running the vitriolic agenda were traced to Pakistan's ISI. As soon as the media got another topic to run 24×7 'Breaking News' ticker, the national mood too changed. Halal meat was back in favour !

Settling scores using COVID-19 as an excuse was not an inter-religious phenomenon alone. The Islamic republic of Saudi Arabia, sealed off the Eastern Qatif province, which is home to a significant minority of Shia population and often at loggers heads with the Sunni-dominated government. Shia pilgrims from the province travel to Iran for pilgrimage to the holy shrines in Qom and Mashhad even though it is illegal, a justification used by Saudi Government to seal the province, blaming its regional rival Iran for spreading the virus in the Middle East. Suspending entry and exit from Qatif deprived the Shias of visiting holy shrines in Najaf and Karbala in bordering Iraq as well.

Similar discrimination played out against the minority Shias in Sunni-dominated Bahrain too. Bahrain, a staunch enemy of Iran, accused Iran of inciting the Bahraini Shias against the Bahrain Government. As a result, close to a thousand Shia pilgrims visiting the holy city of Mashhad, home to the shrine of the eighth Shia Imam, Ali Ibn Musa-al Ridha got stuck in Iran. The Bahrain Government delayed their return to Bahrain on the pretext of stopping virus spreading into the country and labelling the pilgrims as potential virus carriers.

In Morocco, people across various cities protested and prayed outside mosques to defy an aggressive stance by King Mohammed VI, to close all mosques and prayer gatherings. The protests were galvanised by the Salafist preacher Abu Naim. Moroccan authorities and Salafists have been at logger heads, since the terrorist attack in Casablanca in 2003.


Seldom has the State been able to drastically interfere with religious practices and beliefs. Despite the coexistence, religion always had the upper hand. Even during WW II, most religions remained largely untouched from the fallout of global war. COVID-19 might change the status quo ante.

COVID-19 has impacted all major religions, altering major beliefs, practices and rituals in an unprecedented manner. State directives and guidelines have overtaken religious practices, not for a day or two, but for months now and likely to continue for a long time to come. Be it the holy cities of Mecca, Vatican or Ayodhya, all had to comply with State directives, even if they interfered with the religious beliefs of some.

During Ramnavmi, the final day fasting during Navratri and the birthday of Lord Ram, many people take a holy dip in the River Saryu flowing through the holy city of Ayodhya. On account of COVID-19, no religious event was allowed depriving them of the holy dip. Otherwise, a major religious event with people thronging to religious sermons and temples, remained a subdued affair across India. The long awaited auspicious ceremony of '*bhumi poojan*' for the construction of temple of Lord Ram, too remained a subdued affair on account of COVID-19 restrictions.

Mumbai, the financial capital of India, comes to a standstill during September, for the month-long Ganpati Utsav, with streets reverberating with sounds of drums and religious processions. This year, as the situation exits, it's unlikely to have the same fervour.

State grip over religion has become stronger as social distancing and restricted religious gatherings continue to be the new normal. The state now has full control in implementation and alteration of these norms. Near sweeping power of the state in religious matters is a double-edged sword. On the positive side, it would help implement the guideline to tackle COVID-19 more effectively. On the negative side it may lead to a certain mistrust and allegation of bias against a particular religion or sect, which might divide heterogeneous societies even further.

Religion is best practised in isolation. The conflict occurs when believers make a cohort and try to impose their beliefs on other cohorts with allegiance to another religion or sect. In a way, this period can be termed as the golden period for all regions. Most religions are being practiced in isolation at home, in complete solitude and free from all the ostentations and facade we usually associate with religion. People are doing more charity by helping the less privileged with food and other life essentials. It has given us an opportunity to connect with God, free from all external and often-misguided influences. Cleanliness and hygiene is a common theme across all religions, although practiced in their own unique ways. Hinduism prescribes elaborate rituals to ensure hygiene in everyday life. From child birth ritual of '*Jatakarma*' to the death ritual of '*Anteysthi*,' all focus on cleansing of both the body and the soul. Similarly, the practice of '*Wudhu*' among Muslims, 'Ablution' in Christianity and '*Ishnaan*' in Sikhism, all place high emphasis on cleanliness.

We made the religions complex, entwined them in scriptures, mistook rituals as being spiritual and divided them in idols and symbols we deemed fit. We mistook medium as the message, preachers as Gods and vices with verses. From a spiritual perspective, this tiny virus could be the much-researched God particle, here to reform our astray ways of being human.

On a more worldly note, it appears COVID-19 has the power to alter religions for good. A case in point is the Islamic Jihad, being fathomed by few as a religious act. With the slump in global economy, the flow of petro dollars from oil rich Middle Eastern economies fuelling and funding of Islamic Jihadists would eventually dry up. Even the US is drifting its military strategy from being Middle East centric to China centric. The diversion of funds from military to immediate healthcare needs and measures to revive national economies is likely to choke up the lifeline of these groups. Even states which support these groups as strategic assets have no major motivation to use them as the world remains focused on tackling the pandemic. For the Jehadists as well, there is no fun in living on the edge when the world media is busy covering the pandemic 24X7. At least, in the short term, the pandemic can turn the world into a peaceful place.

In a world rife with religious extremism of the worst kind, COVID-19 might bring in the much-needed reform in the way we practice religion. Some say that COVID-19 is an act of God to punish mankind. Punish or not, it is indeed an act of God which has the power to reform us. Only if we are able to decode the message from the divine, enshrined in this catastrophe.

# CHAPTER EIGHT

## WARFARE Vs WELFARE

In anticipation of a full-blown conventional war with its adversaries, countries around the world have been investing heavily in ramping up their military capabilities. A significant portion of their GDP is invested in purchasing conventional weapons, transport and surveillance equipment, maintaining defence forces and intelligence networks. Investment in defence and military is based on the threat perception by each country from its adversaries, i.e. both state and non-state actors, and may not necessarily have any bearing on its economic status, length of its international borders or the size of its population. Saudi Arabia with a population of 34 million spends close to 9% of its GDP on defence. Oman, with a much smaller population of 5 million, is not far behind with 8% of its GDP spent on defence. Israel, situated in middle of not-so-friendly neighbourhood and a population of 8 million, spends 5% of its GDP on defence. China and India, the two largest countries by population, spend 1.9% and 2.4% of their GDP respectively on defence. Pakistan spends close to 4% and the US close to 3.4%.

Every sovereign nation has the right to decide on its defence budget based on its geopolitical interests. That's not the moot point here. The unfortunate story begins when nations entangle themselves in non-essential conflicts so deep that more pressing priorities such as healthcare and public welfare take a backseat. Countries like Saudi Arabia, India, Pakistan and Oman are examples where defence spending is much larger than healthcare spending as a percentage of GDP – a clear case of misplaced priority, especially, when a large section of their population struggles to get basic healthcare and sanitation facilities.

Defence spending has often been associated with national pride and might of a nation, helping politicians win popular support. A display of military paraphernalia and the news surrounding acquisition of fighter aircrafts, submarines, tanks and missiles make international headlines and sway public opinion. Ironically, in recent history, the so-called military deterrence has not been of much use either. The US, despite its military might, had to make a sorry retreat from Vietnam. It failed miserably on 9/11, despite having one of the best-equipped intelligence networks, and spent ten years searching for its biggest enemy, Osama Bin Laden, who was hiding in the backyard of its once-trusted ally, Pakistan. In post COVID-19 world, the irony is likely to become even more relevant. It could bring a paradigm shift in the way nations look at their defence priorities, military or otherwise.

In the aftermath of 9/11, for almost two decades, the US foreign and defence policy has revolved around the Middle East. Its failure to catch Bin Laden drove US to Iraq from Afghanistan. Internal conflicts after the fall of Saddam Hussein and the US' inability to manage the civil strife led them to exit Iraq, thereby creating an ecosystem for organizations like Islamic State to flourish. Dalliance with Iran over the nuclear deal complicated matters further for them in the Middle East, bringing them closer to a full scale war with Iran, just a few months before COVID-19 happened. US entanglement in the Middle East has often been attributed to its oil interests. With significant domestic oil reserves and crude prices in an abyss, involvement in Middle East has lost its economic relevance for the US.

Think tanks in US are already of the opinion that US fixation with counter terrorism is not commensurate with the cost of its engagement in Middle East. As per a report from the Watson Institute of International and Public Affairs at Brown University, USA has spent $6.4 trillion of taxpayers' money since 2001 in various conflicts in Iraq, Afghanistan, Pakistan, Syria and other regions in the Middle East with little gains for its stated goals of finding Weapons of Mass Destruction (WMD) or countering global terrorism.

President Trump, for all his rhetoric, appears logical to the average American taxpayers. He has already announced withdrawal of troops from Afghanistan and Syria and reduced anti-terrorism aid to its long-time ally, Pakistan.

Post COVID-19, public opinion in the US will be focussed inwards, forcing policy makers to address the domestic concerns on unemployment, economic revival, restructuring its global supply chain and strengthening its health care system to prepare for any future pandemics. COVID-19 crisis is going to reorient the average US citizen's and policymakers' outlook of the outer world. This will have a domino effect on foreign policy of not just US, but all major countries in the world.

In its pre-occupation with counter terrorism and conflicts in Middle East, US has ignored the economic rise of China and the intrusion it has made in the life of an average American. Thanks to Trump's obsession with origin of the virus and its economic impact in post COVID-19 era, that is going to change. US foreign and defence policy is likely to now revolve around China, which, in itself, is enough to tweak many other global partnerships, be it in trade, defence or international relations.

President Trump, who is seeking re-election in end of 2020, will use his "Kung Flu" storyline to further his domestic agenda. He is likely to get the support from American voters desperately looking for a leader who is seemingly more nationalist and promotes indigenous industry, thereby creating more employment and an economy which is insulated to such pandemics and their after effects.

Amid the increasing rift between the two countries, the US has upped the ante against strategic and commercial Chinese interests in the US. On 22nd May, 2020, the US Senate passed a bill which would bar Chinese companies such as Alibaba Group Holding Ltd. and Baidu Inc. from listing on US bourses. The bill was approved by unanimous consent from both Republican and Democrat congressmen.

The bill would require companies to certify that they are not under the control of a foreign government. If a company is not able to show that it is not under such control or the Public Company Accounting Oversight Board isn't able to audit the company for three consecutive years to determine if the said company is under foreign government control or not, the company's securities would be banned from the exchanges.

The growing concern in US emanates from the fact that billions of dollars flowing into large Chinese corporations is coming from US pension funds and college endowments. One of the major concerns is the growing clout of Chinese firms funded by American money in the field of artificial intelligence and data collection, exposing Americans interests to manipulation by China.

In a similar instance of escalating animosity between the two economic powers, a bill to sanction Chinese officials over human rights abuses against Muslim minorities in China was passed recently. The US has made its intention clear of taking China head-on, by reviving its vocal support to Taiwan. It first supported Taiwan's attempt to participate in World Health Assembly meeting and then, congratulated Taiwanese President Tsai Ing-wen on her re-election, provoking ire from China. It also waded into the Sino-Indian border dispute, calling Chinese intrusions as dangerous, drawing much retribution from China.

The escalating US - China confrontation which has intensified with COVID-19, is likely to change the course of global geo-politics in the coming decades, much like the Cold War between US and Russia did. Let's call it 'The Red War,' as it involves communist China. The Red War will be fundamentally different from the Cold War, as the potent weapons used in this war will be economic rather than military.

China seems to have an early lead in the war with its investment clout in African and Asian countries, OBOR initiative and allies like Russia, North Korea, Iran and all-weather friend, Pakistan. It has been strengthening its clout on international forums and making new friendships in the Middle East. As per The New York Times, China is planning a comprehensive military and trade partnership with Iran, worth $400 billion investments over next twenty- five years. It could pave way for Chinese military bases in Iran, fundamentally changing the region's geopolitics.

The US is on shaky ground with its battered economy and fragile friendships in Europe and Asia. Its disregard for international institutions and alliances under the leadership of President Trump may further act to its disadvantage. However, the US still has an edge with its massive economic clout and strong institutions, experienced in manipulating any situation, as per their own interests.

The economic cost of the pandemic is likely to squeeze the US GDP by a massive 40% and push unemployment rates as high as 30%. To stem further erosion of a sinking economy, the US has already announced a $3 trillion stimulus package. As per estimates, the US economy might not get back to pre-COVID-19 levels until 2023, and total losses over the next decade could be as high as $19 trillion. With a massive national debt of $24 trillion, increased spending and loss of tax revenues, this stimulus package has to make its way by eating into the defence spending.

It is not the US alone which will be forced to cut its defence spending. The world's largest military alliance, NATO, is also likely to cut its defence spending owing to increase in public expenditure by member states due to the pandemic. It comes at a time when US was pushing member states to contribute up to 2% of their GDP to the alliance's defence budget.

South Korea announced curtailing it defence budget by 2% ($ 740 million) owing to diversion of funds to disaster relief and economic stimulus. A similar announcement was made by Thailand, cutting its defence budget by 8% ($560 million).

As the pandemic progresses, more countries are likely to follow suit as they dole out stimulus packages to revive economic activity, which had come to a standstill during the lockdowns. India, the world's 3rd largest military spender and second largest arms importer, launched a whopping $270 billion stimulus package to revive its economy. Obviously, the funds have to flow in by cutting on other major expense heads, which, in most likelihood, would be defence. Saudi Arabia is the world's 5th largest defence spender and the largest importer of defence equipment. Given the global slump in oil demand and with crude prices at an all-time low, cutting on its defence spending seems to be the only option Saudi Arabia has at the moment.

The only country expected to buck the trend is China, which is predicted to moderately increase its defence spending by at least 3%. Its rising confrontation with US, a vocal Taiwan defying the "One China" policy, border conflict with India, protests in Hong Kong and a volatile South China Sea are believed to be the drivers of its increased defence spending.

Global emergency spending due to the pandemic is expected to cost world economy 9.5% of global output, besides leaving many countries in massive debts. Political leadership in most countries would be under severe pressure to spend a larger sum on social security and healthcare, and less on defence.

In the global war against the virus, weapons stand to lose out to weeping economies. And that possibly could bring elusive peace to many conflict zones in the world, with diversion of funds where they are needed the most, i.e public welfare.

# CHAPTER NINE

## HAWLEY RETURNS

The pandemic has caused an economic mayhem worldwide. Lockdowns and closed international borders have dealt a body blow to global trade and commerce like never before, especially in sectors such as Aviation, Tourism, Hospitality, Retail, Lifestyle and Leisure. International air passenger traffic has reduced to a bare minimum, with only evacuation flights by national carriers functioning to ferry back stranded citizens. The number of scheduled flights worldwide during the first week of May 2020 had declined by 70% as compared to same period in 2019. Back of the envelope forecasts suggest a 13-32% decline in merchandise trade, 30-40% reduction in foreign direct investment and an unprecedented drop of 44-80% in international airline passengers in 2020 due to COVID-19.

Even before the pandemic started, the world economy was going through a rough patch, chequered with the rising nationalist sentiment across countries, strains of global geo-politics, oil crisis, the US-China trade war and modest growth in emerging economies led by China and India. COVID-19 added the extra zing to the prevailing turmoil, catapulting it into a full blown economic catastrophe.

Over the last three decades, international trade had become more globalised with lower barriers to entry, easing access to global markets. Innovation in communication, transportation and manufacturing fuelled this growth in global trade which has almost tripled from $6.5 trillion in 2000 to $19.5 trillion in 2018. Global free trade, which was the guiding mantra behind this growth and transformation of global economy, is now under threat, given the clamour to protect domestic industry and impetus on self-reliance. Rising protectionism the world over has already caused the Brexit in Europe, fuelled the US - China trade war, made the US recast NAFTA into the United States–Mexico–Canada Agreement (USMCA) and withdraw from Trans Pacific Partnership negotiations. More recently, it was one of the reasons behind India pulling out of the Regional Comprehensive Economic Partnership (RCEP) at the eleventh hour.

As the COVID-19 crisis unfolded, countries witnessed side effects of an economic eco-system having high dependence on global supply chains. The pandemic caused critical shortages of essential equipment and materials, exposing healthcare systems in countries to fragile global supply chain models which until now did not build any safeguards to tackle such pandemics and the ensuing challenges. The fact that China has a significant leverage in global trade due to its dominance in manufacturing, further complicated matters.

China is the largest source of goods exported around the world, while its current adversary, the US, also happens to be its biggest export destination. Since 2018, the trade deficit between US and China has been declining, and during COVID-19, it has come down to its lowest level.

It is further going to reduce, driven by President Trump's 'America First' policy and his compulsions to keep his core support base in good stead, which has been struggling with an unprecedented hike in unemployment rates. This tectonic shift in trade equations between two economic superpowers will create long-enduring ripples across global trade.

Learning from the COVID-19 experience, countries now have to either diversify their supply chains or need to bring back manufacturing into their home country. It is a fundamental shift in economic wisdom of policy makers worldwide, as COVID-19 crisis has exposed two major shortcomings of global trade – first being the over-reliance on one country for all manufacturing needs and second, outsourcing of manufacturing to cheaper destinations, that killed domestic jobs.

Professor Theodore Levitt of the Harvard Business School would be recoiling in his grave with disgust, realizing that the term 'globalisation' which he coined, may not remain the much fancied term any more, as it has been during the last three decades.

Bruised industries are relying on stimulus packages to bail them out. Incentives, tax concessions and cash doles to spur consumer spending is already putting a strain on national exchequers. As a result, the role and influence of governments on public sentiment is at an all-time high. Corporates, SMEs, individuals, trade associations and financial institutions are all looking up to the government to bail them out.

The situation creates an ideal ground for governments to push through populist economic reforms, impose trade and non-trade barriers to protect domestic industry and create more employment opportunities.

On the 12th of May, 2020, India's Prime Minister, Narendra Modi, announced a mega economic revival package worth $270 billion. The package had major thrust on 'self-reliance' (*atma-nirbhar*) with incentives for small businesses and domestic manufacturing. It was one of the most-substantial revival packages, equal to 10% of India's GDP announced by any developing country. In GDP percentage terms, only Japan, US, Australia and Germany rolled out a larger stimulus than India, which stood at 21%, 13%, 10.8% and 10.7% of their GDP, respectively. India was presumably the most vocal in highlighting the thrust on self-reliance among the major global economies.

The impetus on self-reliance, although aimed at strengthening domestic industry with focus on manufacturing and job creation, for proponents of global trade, it can be construed as return of protectionism. Such apprehensions are not entirely out of context either. Even though the Indian Government clarified it does not mean boycott of foreign goods and brands, soon after the announcement, social media was abuzz with messages to boycott foreign goods and brands and especially, products made in China.

The self-reliance package unveiled by India echoed a similar popular sentiment prevailing globally. Japan's COVID-19 stimulus includes subsidies for firms that repatriate factories. The European Union is talking about "strategic autonomy," and is creating a fund to buy stakes in firms. America is urging Intel to build manufacturing plants at home.

As they say, history repeats itself. The Spanish Flu pandemic in early 1920s was followed by the Great Depression of the 1930s, which saw an increase in protectionist trade policies, economic hardships and rise of nationalism in most countries, which eventually led to the World War II.

One of the causes attributed to the Great Depression was the enactment of The Smoot–Hawley Tariff Act, which raised US tariffs on over 20,000 imported goods. This act was the brainchild of Senator Reed Smoot and Representative Willis C. Hawley, both Republicans from Utah and Oregon, respectively. The main goal of the act was to protect the jobs and farmers in US from foreign competition, as rapid industrialization was making more people jobless. The use of motorised transport, on the other hand, was freeing up more land for agriculture, otherwise used for grazing by horses and mules, thereby causing an increase in domestic agricultural productivity. The incomes, however, did not rise proportionally, leading to oversupply and lesser demand in the US. To address this, Congressmen Smoot and Hawley advocated that raising the tariff on imports would alleviate the overproduction problem. In reality, the United States was actually running a trade account surplus, as manufactured goods exports were growing faster.

The act met with severe retaliation from US trading partners, even before if came into effect in 1930, with imposition of tariffs on imports from the US imposed by some of its major trading partners – Canada, Britain, Germany and France, eventually plunging the global trade by 67% during 1929 to 1934.

Interestingly, ninety years after start of the Great Depression, another Republican, Senator Josh Hawley from Missouri, wrote an article in The New York times, demanding World Trade Organisation (WTO) to be abolished, and for the US to exit the global trade body as a first step towards it. His main argument is that the interest of US workers and farmers have suffered at the cost of steady rise of China, and WTO has failed to protect US interests. Stoking nationalist American sentiments, he says, "Now is the time to return production back in America to secure critical supply chains and encourage domestic innovation and manufacturing."

His rant against the WTO may not be misplaced, if viewed from an average American's point of view, but for global trade, it does sounds a like a death knell. WTO is already facing an existential crisis. The ongoing US - China trade war could lead to collapse of the global trade body. At the time of global crises, when it is needed the most, the collapse of the WTO could lead to a free-for-all and global economic debauchery.

Global trade would suffer as countries in their pursuit of building self-resilient economy would be inclined to look the other way when it comes to treating goods and services equally, regardless of their origins. Governments and central banks are protecting domestic firms by using taxpayer's money via stimulus packages, which creates a long-term commitment to favour them.

In words of former WTO Chief Pascal Lamy, "The world will face more governments, more precautions, less growth, more digital, more inequalities among countries and fewer inequalities within countries."

Retreating from global trade might be a good political gimmick to keep masses on your side, but in the long run, the benefits of globalisation may outwit misplaced fears. Retaliatory tariffs and non-tariff barriers, increased cost of goods, restricted technology transfer, subdued innovation, reduced movement of people and goods will eventually square off the gains made by inward movement of jobs and manufacturing.

Adverse economic impact of COVID-19 is a reality and so is the fact that we will bounce back. When we do bounce back, however, the global market place may not look the same. Months of lockdowns have changed consumer habits, preferences and spending patterns. Lost or reduced incomes, fear of an uncertain future, lack of liquidity, risk aversion, focus on automation and digitalization are some factors which would transform global trade in post COVID-19 era. Future demands that borders and minds need to remain open for global trade to prosper.

Globalisation has fostered economic and social well-being in many countries. Both rich and poor nations have reaped its benefits. The gains transcended not just the economic spectrum, but also to other human development parameters in education, health, environment and social well-being. During the last thirty years of globalisation, China and India have moved close to one billion people out of poverty. Thanks to globalization, a Least Developed Country (LDC) like Bangladesh has been growing at more than 6% annually in the last decade, bringing one third of its population out of poverty and expects to graduate out of its LDC status by 2024.

Recoiling against globalization would mean dismantling existing economic networks and scrapping the associated investments. It would make a bad situation much, much worse. Short-term and short-sighted gains may become penury of the future.

History repeats itself for a purpose. The purpose this time around is to remind us of not succumbing to Hawley's folly again!

# CHAPTER TEN

## THE CATHARSIS

Catastrophes, man-made or God sent, play an integral part in human evolution. They are a consequence of the interactions we humans make with other stakeholders of the universe. The catharsis leads to a transformation, which eventually becomes an essential part of our lives, psyche and culture.

World War II changed the narrative of human history. Most prominent among the changes brought about by the global war was the creation of United Nations and its several off shoots. On the geo-political front, it sowed seeds of the Cold War. On the technology front, it gave us the radars, first computer prototype – the Colossus and synthetic rubber. Among the lesser known inventions triggered by the war were the super glue, the duct tape, Tupperware and even burgers and sugar coated chocolate pebbles! Post war socio-economic security caused the baby boom across US and Europe. It led to the emancipation of countries like India, Indonesia and The Philippines from clutches of colonial exploitation, and resurgence of self-reliant economies like Japan and Germany, which were decimated during the war.

Going further deep into history, the Spanish Flu pandemic caused close to 20 million (6% of then Indian population) deaths in India alone. As per the account of famous Hindi poet, Suryakant Tripathi Nirala, several rivers, including the Ganges, were flooded with dead bodies. Nirala himself lost his close family members, including his wife, to the Spanish Flu. Unlike the British officers, most Indians resided in small, congested houses and neighbourhoods. One of the reasons for high mortality among Indians was the lack of access to healthcare and sanitation facilities. The brazen apathy of British rulers who ignored the plight of poor Indians fuelled resentment against the ruling British empire.

When Mahatma Gandhi launched the non-cooperation movement to protest against the British atrocities, it gained tremendous support from the masses who were already angered by the Jallianwalah Bagh massacre and the conduct of the British regime during the flu pandemic. Grass-root support made non-cooperation a pan India movement, putting British Government on the back foot and Mahatma Gandhi on the front foot as a national leader of the freedom struggle. The countdown to freedom at midnight had just started.

The Spanish flu led to creation of public healthcare systems in Russia and Europe. Disillusioned by allopathy, many in the US turned to alternative medicine. In the then less-evolved China, it led to higher focus on science with impetus on disease surveillance, data collection and public healthcare. As a favourable outcome of the pandemic, there was greater emphasis on development of drugs and vaccines. Although the first flu vaccine could only emerge in 1938, it set the ball rolling. The antibiotic penicillin and vaccines for tuberculosis and polio were launched within the next decade.

One of the most defining behavioural changes brought about by the Spanish Flu was the coughing and sneezing etiquette, which we practice even today and has become so integral to our social behaviour. To promote the cough etiquette, the slogan *"Coughs and Sneezes Spread Diseases"* was widely publicised in United States. It was later adopted by the United Kingdom to encourage good public hygiene and prevent the spread of the common cold, influenza and other respiratory illnesses, making it a common theme across the globe.

Even then, it was not easy for the authorities to convince people into following the cough etiquette, wearing masks and hand washing. Some considered it a violation of their civil liberty and some men considered it feminine to wear masks or to cover their cough!

It required deft advertising with a dash of patriotism and macho-imagery to finally convince the men. Covering one's cough grew into becoming a common courtesy; until the Spanish flu happened, this etiquette was almost unheard of.

Behavioural changes triggered by threats such as the fear of being infected by the virus may not be sustainable in the long term. However, such habits, practiced over time, reduce the chances of them disappearing altogether. The global scare caused by the modern day communication tools and increased avenues for close contact due to wide usage of mass transit systems, malls and cinema halls make

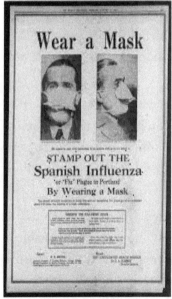

*Source: US Public Health Service Ad, 1918, Public*

COVID-19 even more scarier than the previous pandemics. Although the casualties are much lower, the threat of a higher number persists, as we have no visibility as to when it will end.

The human mind is pre-disposed to assigning more weightage to potential losses than gains while making choices. In evolved societies, these traits can become amplified and obsessive. The fact that there is no vaccine or treatment available for COVID-19 has made people worldwide become more concerned about their health and resort to time-tested methods such as yoga, physical exercise, vegetarianism and a healthy diet to boost immunity. There is renewed interest in alternative therapies like Ayurveda, Homeopathy and Naturopathy.

In the post COVID-19 era, the likelihood of people avoiding public transport, social gatherings and crowded places are much higher. Reduced traffic on city roads due to lockdowns clubbed with the health benefits of cycling has created a new demand for bicycles the world over that was not seen in decades. Cities around the world witnessed bicycle sales zoom manifold, while streets are bustling with bicycle traffic.

Auckland, Bagota, New York City, Philadelphia, Milan, Berlin, London, Paris, Manila and Dhaka have all have seen increase in bicycle ridership, forcing city planners to modify traffic patterns to cope with the surge. Countries are encouraging bike ownership using subsidies. France is providing a $55 subsidy towards the refurbishment of any bicycles available, while Italy has introduced a "bici bonus" of 500 euros, upwards of 60% of the cost, to purchase a bike.

Even in countries like Bangladesh and India, where bicycles were giving way to motorised vehicles, there was a jump in bicycle sales. However, the switch has more to do with survival than the esoteric compulsions of the West. In India, migrant labourers were stuck in cities due to the sudden lockdown. In absence of any public mode of transport to go back to their hometowns and villages, they took to the humble bicycle to ride back home, sometimes as far as 1500 kilometres, causing spike in sales of bicycles, most often purchased by selling meagre belongings or with borrowed money.

Who can forget the grit and determination of Jyoti Kumari – a fifteen year old girl, who peddled more than 1,200 kilometres to bring her ailing father back from Delhi to Darbhanga – all this with her injured father riding pillion!

Adversities do bring out our best. It's all about the choices we make.

'Black Lives Matter' protests triggered by the killing of George Floyd became a global movement to highlight the discrimination of blacks in US and other parts of the world. The high number of casualties among the black population due to the pandemic gave the movement a new lease of life. The issue lying under the carpet so far was re-ignited in the American psyche, and resonated across the globe.

The pandemic has brought to light discrimination of all types back in public discourse. If it was not for the pandemic, it would have been really hard for men to realise the sacrifice and efforts put in by women in managing a household. Months of lockdown had forced people to do all household chores by themselves – mostly, the womenfolk. For working women, it's a double whammy of balancing work and household priorities. The situation is more or less similar across the world, with women taking lead in household work and yet, being unpaid and unrecognized for it.

The gender disparity is higher in conservative societies like the Indian sub-continent. This disparity has become slightly blurred during the pandemic, as families are gradually getting used to sharing household work. The stereotypes of women doing dishes, cooking meals or mopping the floor, being considered female-only tasks, are being broken. It might still be a long transition for these interim changes to develop into habits and lead to changed mind-sets. Subconsciously, a beginning has been made, thanks to the pandemic.

Countries led by women such as Germany, Taiwan, New Zealand, Finland, Norway, Denmark, Singapore and Iceland have all fared well in containing the pandemic, highlighting the expertise of women in managing issues which require compassion and care. Women tend to adopt a more risk-averse approach with regard to human lives, but they are more prepared to take significant risks when it comes to financials. That possibly explains the early decision of these women leaders in locking down their economies as their initial response in containing the virus spread.

Women leaders such as Angela Merkel of Germany, Jacinda Arden from New Zealand, Tsai Ing-wen in Taiwan and Sanna Marin from Finland have garnered global praise for their decisiveness and collaborative style of leadership, and as better communicators – skills crucial in making a connect with the masses while tackling a pandemic.

In our neighbourhood, Bangladesh's Prime Minister, Sheikh Hasina, has been decisively tackling the pandemic, despite leading a nation of 160 million with a large migrant workforce and dense population fraught with religious extremism.

Closer to home, another women leader, K.K Shailaja, Health Minister of Kerala, earned global recognition for her efforts in keeping the mortality rates low, despite her state being densely populated with porous borders and having one of the highest overseas migrant populations.

Women make approximately 70% of the global workforce at the frontlines, fighting the pandemic. In the social sectors and as care givers at home, the contribution of women is remarkable as they dabble between their professional and personal responsibilities.

It is presumably due to the faith in ability of women to manoeuvre out of complex situations that WHO appointed two women – Former Liberian President, Ellen Johnson Sirleaf, a Nobel Peace Prize winner, and Helen Clark, former Prime Minister of New Zealand, to lead an expert panel set up to review WHO's own response and that of its member states on the pandemic.

Women did not lead us into the previous World Wars. Hopefully, neither will they lead us in the future. Yet, all wars of the world being fought to bring peace and prosperity – now and in the future, will never be accomplished without their leadership and skills.

Refugees, asylum seekers, internally-displaced people (IDPs) and migrants are among the worst-impacted people due to the pandemic. Their plight is exacerbated due to the poor living conditions in refugee camps or crammed neighbourhoods with congested living spaces, making social distancing norms "an impossible luxury." Some are even forced to live on streets, out in the open. Most of them lack access to basic services such as clean water, sanitation and access to healthcare. COVID-19 has added to the xenophobia, racism and stigmatization they face in the host regions, while the pandemic continues to shatter their lives and livelihoods. As per UN estimates, the pandemic will cause a drop of $109 billion in remittances which flow from these people to 800 million people who are dependent on it for their survival.

Whether it's a Rohingiya refugee from Myanmar's Rakhine region or the migrant labours from Indian states of UP and Bihar, who move to metro cities in search of a livelihood and possibly a better life, their motivation to move out is common – the lack of earning opportunities in their homeland. This disparity in development caused by years of neglect of local governments, adds not only to the plight of whom it displaces but also creates social, economic and infrastructure challenges for the host regions, thereby causing a vicious cycle of suffering for both hosts and migrants.

It has to change. This pandemic could act as the trigger.

The rising xenophobia and protectionist sentiment prevailing around the world, realignment of global supply chains away from China, focus on indigenous manufacturing and impetus to small and medium scale enterprises can drive a much-needed reverse migration from larger cities to the smaller ones and villages. If (and that's a big IF) the rhetoric culminates into real action, we might witness a halt to mass migration of labour, as more and more cities and hinterlands become developed and prosperous, propelled by the stimulus packages being rolled out by governments.

It's the only way we can ensure prosperity for all. Peace will follow.

Among the many casualties caused by the current crisis are the new age Start-ups. Before the virus unleashed, technology-driven start-ups with disruptive business models were the darling of investors, entrepreneurs and job aspirants alike. Business models of most start-ups relied heavily on rapid customer acquisition, churning out doles of discounts and burning cash in the process. Customers were the king, while entrepreneurs and investors were enjoying the fling.

Suddenly, the pandemic happens. By June, 70% start-ups had terminated their full-time employee contracts and 40% of them were carrying cash to sustain them only for three months or less. A majority of them operated in sectors worst hit during the pandemic, such as urban mobility, hospitality, travel, food delivery and shared spaces. Softbank, one of the major start-up investors worldwide, had to take a $6.6 billion write-down on WeWork and might lose even more as the fundamental business model of WeWork – sitting side by side in close contact with strangers – has now become unthinkable. Urban mobility giants like Uber and Ola are operating at suboptimal levels, as more and more people are avoiding public transport vehicles. Intermittent lockdowns are not helping either.

However, other start-up models such as virtual meeting platforms, medicine delivery, gaming and on-line education are adding customers in hordes, riding on the new reality of our times. Online education start-up BYJUs became a decacorn by surpassing a $10.5 billion valuation after raising new funding from Silicon Valley investor, Bond Capital. It was able to clinch the deal by showcasing to investors the new students it added and extra hours spent by existing students on its platform during the lockdown. It achieved the feat of becoming a decacorn from a unicorn in just two years. Again, thanks to the pandemic.

Not every start-up had a similar dream run. It's a daily battle for survival for most, forcing them to lay-off employees and curtail operations. Current times are an opportunity for entrepreneurs and investors to recalibrate the assumptions, repurpose business model and even make the switch to more sustainable business ideas.

The pandemic experience of high risk – high reward start-up models – could even lead to renewed interest of entrepreneurs in conventional brick and mortar businesses which have a more predictable trajectory. State emphasis on indigenisation could further catalyse the shift from start-ups to more conservative business models. Conventional wisdom may score over fledgling ideas yet again !

The virus outbreak in Wuhan came into public knowledge through a WeChat message from Dr Li to his batch mates. In a way, information technology (IT) had it imprints from day one in the current crisis. On one hand, it has proven a boon in identification and tracking of suspect cases, disease surveillance, spreading awareness, disease management and information exchange between governments, doctors and researchers. On the flip side, it has created panic around the pandemic in most countries. Social media is flooded with memes, videos, articles and blogs which are most often a concoction of fact and fiction, compounding the catastrophe. Authorities around the world are dealing with two challenges – Corona Pandemic and Corona Infodemic .

In absence of the new age information technology tools available to us today, the impact of COVID-19 on human lives and economy could have been debilitating. Data analytics and Artificial Intelligence is helping researchers find a potential cure and vaccine candidates by analysing disease outcomes. At the same time, other information technology tools such as virtual meeting platforms, digital entertainment and grocery delivery apps are ensuring that we have what we need to stay home, keeping us safe and secure.

Information technology is indeed a double-edged sword. It can put our privacy at risk and up for manipulation. Governments can keep a hawk eye on its citizens, while other vested interests can use personal data for their ulterior motives. The pandemic offers a perfect setting to do this. Use of drones to identify people violating lockdowns, and GPS and facial recognition to track and trace potential COVID-19 carriers have been used effectively during the pandemic. The database so created could be more lethal than any weapon of mass destruction available, if used with malicious intent by hackers or a hostile nation. The *brouhaha* against 5G provider Huawei or TikTok is not without a reason after all.

The pandemic has just helped us unearth a Weapon of Mass Destruction (WMD) which has been strategically positioned in our hands. Beware!

The seemingly biggest beneficiary of the pandemic has been Mother Nature. Restricted flight movement and road traffic, closure of tourist destinations and beaches and low industrial activity has led to a positive impact on the environment. During the initial days of lockdown, pollution in New York was reduced by nearly 50%; in China, emissions fell 25% at the start of the year. Satellite images showed nitrogen dioxide (NO2) emissions fading away over northern Italy during peak of pandemic fury in the country. Images of the Himalayan ranges being visible from Indian cities situated a hundred miles away due to reduced air pollution were a soothing treat to eyes. River Ganges saw a decline in pollution levels reduced by half. Another, major Indian river, the Yamuna, turned azure during the initial days of the lockdown.

Unfortunately, most of these changes were short lived. Yet, the pandemic gave nature an opportunity to breathe fresh air, do repairs to the depleted ozone layer and rekindle flora and fauna in the jungles and oceans while mankind struggles for survival. The pandemic has shown that nature is keen to make amends and will respond fast to our efforts. The onus to oblige lies on us.

As and when the pandemic retracts, these short terms gains might vanish. Rise in traffic of individual motorised vehicles, increased used of soap, sanitizers and disinfectants polluting rivers, glut of bio-hazardous waste and lenient environmental clearances in the backdrop of manufacturing push could be potentially detrimental to cause of the environment. They may reverse the minor gains we might have made effortlessly, during the pandemic.

It might be premature to claim a victory on this front, as neither we can claim credit for the momentary gains, nor can we expect the pandemic to reoccur and repeat the fluke.

Nature has its own unique ways of finding equilibrium. Since we haven't obliged, it has found one on its own – COVID-19.

This pandemic has forced us to value beliefs and practices we abandoned, considering them archaic and outdated. Our minds were so clouded by commerce that we lost common sense. In pursuit to unlock value, we have bartered old values.

COVID-19 has taught us all that we forgot – be it following cleanliness and hygiene, social etiquettes, maintaining a healthy lifestyle, spending time with family, faith in the power of supreme, following the rule of law or self-discipline. The old adage of *'Prevention is better than cure'* seems so much more relevant today. It is possibly the only way we can save ourselves from the wrath of the virus.

It would be naive to guess if the world post COVID-19 will change for better or worse. Altering our own beliefs and actions can, however, deliver more predictable outcomes.

This pandemic is nature's pun. For the rest of us, the catharsis has just begun!

CPSIA information can be obtained
at www.ICGtesting.com
Printed in the USA
BVHW031030290920
589853BV00001B/49